£1-50

45
9/85

MURDER OF A MODERATE MAN

'There's brandy somewhere,' said Laleh as she opened the front door. 'I think I need its medicinal effect.' She led Morgan into the sitting room, turned on the light and closed the curtains. A floorboard creaked upstairs as the intruder withdrew across the landing to use the spiral stairs at the back of the house. Morgan looked up at the ceiling.

'Don't worry,' said Laleh. 'It's an old house. It creaks and groans sometimes.' She poured two brandies, handed one to Morgan and shivered. 'It's cold.'

They were standing close, looking at each other. Morgan reached out a hand to touch her face. Laleh took a step forward into his arms, her head down on his shoulder, a hand round the back of his head.

'Hold me,' she whispered, and turned her face towards his mouth.

Then froze suddenly like a block of stone staring over his shoulder at the pair of eyes and hooded head watching them through the partition.

D0306309

MURDER OF A MODERATE MAN

John Howlett

Arrow Books

For Parviz Z. and
the countless thousands
under most regimes.

Arrow Books Limited
17–21 Conway Street, London W1P 6JD
An imprint of the Hutchinson Publishing Group
London Melbourne Sydney Auckland
Johannesburg and agencies throughout
the world

First published in Great Britain 1985

© John Howlett 1985

The translation of 'Earth
Poem' by Mahmoud Darwish is by
kind permission of
Bassim Musallam.

This book is sold subject to the condition that it shall not,
by way of trade or otherwise, be lent, resold, hired out,
or otherwise circulated without the publisher's prior
consent in any form of binding or cover other than that
in which it is published and without a similar condition including this condition being imposed on the
subsequent purchaser

Photoset in Linotron Bembo by
Rowland Phototypesetting Limited
Bury St Edmunds, Suffolk
Printed and bound in Great Britain by
Anchor Brendon Limited, Tiptree, Essex

ISBN 0 09 941850 9

PROLOGUE

In contrast with how the others were to die, old Vaziree died a clean and simple death. A little girl in the crowded airport held out a bunch of flowers; Vaziree stooped to take them; the girl, either frightened or shy, dropped the flowers; Vaziree stooped further to pick them up. A gun appeared from under a robe behind him, the barrel placed to the back of his neck. Vaziree sprawled forward in a sudden spasm, the flowers scattering again across the floor.

The giant Farshid afterwards likened Vaziree's death to a routine killing in a small provincial slaughterhouse – 'a frail and ageing bull,' he wrote, 'buckling at the knees with the slaughterer's bolt.' At the time, Farshid had cried like a child and folded Parviz into a bear-like hug as though to shield him.

Parviz remembered it in a series of confused images: a giant two-bladed fan turning slowly above them all; the girl with the bunch of flowers; the background voices in the crowd calling his father's name. Parviz was talking to Annie when he heard the gun, and all he saw as he turned were the flowers scattering on the floor and the red spreading stain on his father's white robe. Parviz Vaziree came to re-live that moment each time he woke from sleep, reminding himself every morning that his father was no longer there to guide him and the party with stern and careful wisdom.

Nor did the little girl's memory fade too easily. The police interrogated her for days afterwards in an attempt to discover who had placed the flowers in her hand, refusing to believe she'd picked them herself. 'From the gardens of Isfahan,' she'd been told to whisper as Vaziree stooped and smiled at her.

The assassin's own recollection was brutal and short, overshadowed by what he immediately recognized as his own betrayal. Two men placed ready to chase him knew exactly where a car was meant to be waiting for him. The car itself had disappeared. The two men caught him, one of them pinning him to a wall, the other shooting him four times in the back of the head.

For many that double killing signalled the end of what could have been called the legitimate political resistance.

PART ONE

'Occupation Democrat . . .'

1

Six years and a religious revolution had passed since then. Of his friends and colleagues at that airport shooting, Parviz had no idea how many were still alive. His own survival was a mystery to him, his address – 'somewhere in the Dasht-e-Kavir' – unknown even to Amnesty International.

That 'somewhere' was an old caravanserei, half-ruined and barbed-wired, where the inmates lived on chicken-wire bunks in chicken-wire enclosures, none of them in a fit state to even contemplate escape, if escape two hundred desert miles from nowhere was any kind of temptation beyond suicide.

Tonight they heard the chopper arrive, landing on the ridge as it always did in darkness, the black Toyota running the visitors or newcomers down the track and into the camp.

'*Nacht und Nebel,*' Parviz muttered to himself and listened to the terror of every prisoner waiting for transfer or execution. Once, at night, four men had arrived and by daybreak an entire hut of fifty-six souls had disappeared, gun-shattered skeletons, it was rumoured, somewhere in a dry-stone wadi.

Parviz froze and every man with him in the chicken-wire coop as they heard their own padlock being unlocked, each pair of eyes wide open in the darkness. Those prisoners sitting or squatting on the ground turned in fear to watch the swagger of two boy-soldiers, one at the gate, one moving round the tiers of chicken-wire bunks. For three years Parviz had been waiting for execution or something worse, each sunrise and sunset of those three years asking himself why they had so carefully preserved him for so long.

Tonight it *was* his turn. He felt, as he'd known he would one night feel, two hands grasp his legs and a shoulder and pull him roughly off the wire down onto the dirt and straw of the floor. His legs buckled as the soldier pulled him to his feet and he was pushed across the floor towards the second soldier at the open door, glimpsing the Baha'i boy who'd been his only friend watching him with soulful eyes, the poor little 'Jewish gofer' who'd now be misused and abused by the harder men without Parviz there to hold his corner.

The two young soldiers marched Parviz into the stone corridor and past the soldiers' quarters to the inner sanctum where the commander lived. Parviz wanted to shake off his escorts and stand to walk on his own, feeling that whatever lay ahead of him his own dignity was the first strength he needed. Instead, the boy-soldiers seemed determined to deliver him like the wounded animal he was, the elder of them tripping one foot to make him stumble as he crossed the threshold into the office.

Then Parviz saw the blond head and European arrogance that turned to watch his entrance, and he knew he wasn't yet going to die.

2

Morgan rolled off the couchette into a grey early morning too late to track down the smell of coffee from the back of the train. He shaved in the corridor while the sleeping-cars and couchettes threaded slowly past the Bois de Vincennes.

Morgan hadn't been back to Paris for nine months and was not in the best of moods. Summoned from his pensione in Lugano by police telex at seven o'clock on Saturday evening, he'd had barely an hour to collate the information requested, throw some clothes into a bag and climb the hill from Frau Luethi's to the station. He'd changed stations and trains in Milan, found no sleeping-berths vacant on the *Galilei* and settled for a shared two-up and two-down as the only alternative, three snoring companions undisturbed by his intrusion.

The Gare de Lyon, chilly and empty on a Sunday morning, did nothing to dispel his sleepless gloom. Morgan, with donkey jacket, black canvas bag, and a stern and craggy face, turned away from a long taxi queue and stood brooding at the bar with grainy French espresso and a croissant. Sunday was a bad day to lose in Lugano. The banks were quiet and he would have been at the computer in his underground hutch by now, running through entry codes and a list of accounts, checking on the week's figures, trying to identify the movements of 'laundry funds' and 'blood money' – an activity very *non grata* with the Swiss authorities, who

11

had only the vaguest idea what Morgan was up to in his basement office.

'*Deliver Sunday morning o nine thirty*,' the telex had said. '*Info Veltri finance laundry oil and arms.*'

It had to be Elgin; the bachelor Elgin, who loved to set logistical problems and sabotage weekends. Though he had judged his timetables too fine for Sunday taxis, and it was well past ten o'clock before the Citroën turned up the hill at St Cloud to deposit Morgan outside Interpol's squat rectangle of reflecting windows and roof-top radio aerials.

The office seemed empty, the iron-grille gate opening with a click once Morgan had flashed his unsmiling face and card at the video camera. Opened by a ghost. Reception, stairs and corridors were deserted. The one-way glass looked north over the hillside of gardened residences, south over the railway and the Paris skyline. Morgan imagined Parisian families walking their dogs or children in that vast green sprawl of the Bois de Boulogne.

Elgin's room was also empty, the old man doubtless creating some *mise-en-scène* for the meeting. Probably boiling a bloody kettle, thought Morgan, and knocked on the table calling for 'shop!' over the office partition. And sure enough Elgin plus teapot, tea-cosy and china cups sidled out.

'Nice of you to come, Morgan.'

'On a Sunday.'

Elgin set the teapot down and waved his hand at the outer office: 'Sundays have their advantages. Empty offices. No ears to listen.'

'And a twenty-minute taxi queue at the station.' Morgan pulled a file out of his bag and laid it on the desk. 'I could have had that sent by courier.'

Elgin tapped his teapot: 'Brewing – I'm a five-minute man myself.'

Elgin's Englishness was exaggerated to the point of caricature, perhaps the only way he could survive in such a French-orientated organization. Elgin turned the newspaper on his desk towards Morgan, a mugshot and a headline: MISSING ITALIAN BUSINESSMAN ARRESTED IN BIRMINGHAM. 'Mr Veltri,' said Elgin, picking up Morgan's file. 'What have *you* got on him?'

'Not much. He launders money, but that's been on file for a long time.'

'Where does the money come from?'

'Can't tell. Isn't that the point of laundering?'

'Nothing on armaments?'

Morgan shook his head. 'He's been evading Italian income tax. That's hardly a crime worthy of your attention.'

Elgin tapped the headline in the newspaper. 'Chummy was arrested for travelling on a false passport in the UK and the Italians have already applied for extradition on charges of arms trafficking.' Elgin looked over the desk at Morgan. 'They're expecting you there tomorrow.'

'I told you, I have nothing for them.'

Elgin took a red box-file from a drawer in his desk and pushed it across the desk at Morgan. 'Can't make head nor tail of it myself. Thought you might like a crack. It'd make a change from bank computers.'

Morgan opened the file on pictures and news-cuttings of Veltri.

'He tried to take over where Mattei left off, making private oil deals with the Arabs and the Russians. Didn't go down too well with the Seven Sisters.'

Morgan looked suitably blank. 'The Seven Sisters?'

'The major oil companies, Morgan. The cartel. If you believe in the conspiracy theory, they had Mattei blown up in his private plane. So they weren't too pleased when Veltri tried to muscle in on the same rubber. The Marco Polo tradition. Come to think of it, they were all Italians, the ones who caused the major damage. Marco Polo discovered China, and we surely could have done without the Orient. Then Columbus found America, for

13

which he certainly should have been excommunicated.'

Morgan smiled politely at his jokes. 'I know nothing about oil and even less about armaments. Why send for me?'

'Pure coincidence, Morgan. It's Sunday. There's no one else around.'

'Come on, Elgin. They're all out there somewhere at the end of the telephone, young, energetic, ambitious, knowledgeable. All the qualities you could not expect from me.'

'Experienced?'

'That's not the reason.'

Elgin poured two cups of tea, grey as it hit the milk. He looked again at Morgan and tapped his nose. 'First question: who tipped off Birmingham police that Veltri was travelling on false papers?'

'He'd been missing for a week. His name and face had been circulated.'

'Question two: who's corroborating the charge of arms trafficking against Veltri?' Elgin leant across the table and flicked over pages of the file to turn up another name: Parviz Vaziree, with a list of scribbled dates and places, and eventually a photograph – a likeness dating back a few years to the white shirt and tie of the successful young politician, not the ragged skeleton in the desert prison. 'A political prisoner,' said Elgin. 'Four days ago I told the Italians there was no way even to talk with him. Last night one of our colleagues sprung him.' Elgin looked at his watch. 'At this very moment in time they'll be sitting at Mehrabad, waiting for a flight to London.'

Morgan was staring at Parviz's face on the file, trying to place the vaguely familiar name. It was a strong and serious face with a careful frown; he looked as if he would need to believe in whatever he was doing.

'They've never been known before to release prisoners, even on a temporary basis.' Elgin sipped at his tea. 'He's being brought to testify in Birmingham. If you, Morgan, were to hover with the file? A watching

14

brief? Try to quantify the extent and nature of our involvement.'

'Whose territory would I be trespassing on?'

'Josef Dorff.'

Morgan remembered an impetuous and rather unpleasant German policeman, who had partnered him once in Munich, staking out a Baader–Meinhof suspect. 'I thought he worked from Wiesbaden.'

Elgin nodded. 'Odd, isn't it? The pretext for his involvement is German interest in Veltri as a possible source of weapons for terrorist groups. Veltri was flying from Germany when he was arrested at Birmingham Airport.' Elgin was watching Morgan's doubtful face. 'Birmingham, England; not Alabama, Morgan. You'd be going home.'

3

The airport at Mehrabad was as near as Parviz would ever be to home, ten miles as the vulture flies to the house and garden on the northern outskirts of Teheran where he'd spent his childhood. Not that he had parent, brother or sister any more to call it home.

He seemed to have slept for hours, sedated after a doctor had examined him, eventually locked into a small room far from the airport halls where he might have caused a nuisance – or been recognized. Not that there was much left to recognize. He'd looked into a mirror for the first time in three years and had not known himself: greying hair over a hollow face and eyes that had sunk away.

In the sunset they had walked him out to the plane and up steps, past a hostess in a *chador* at the cabin door whose professional welcome recoiled when she smelt his ragged clothes. He was sat apart and settled with his escort long before the other passengers came on board, two *chadors* now watching them down the aisle wondering who on earth he could be. More likely they were eyeing his European escort. He was handsome enough in a blond, Teutonic way.

This Herr Dorff spoke accented English and referred to himself as a representative of Interpol. Parviz should have felt safer with him than with the boy-soldiers in that desert prison, but his concept of safety had been measured too long within the parameter of his chicken-wire cell. Everything that had happened beyond the open door was unknown and dangerous: the mutterings and signing of papers between the soldiers and this German policeman; the black Toyota toiling back up the ridge to the helicopter silhouetted against the night sky; the whiplash sound of the rotors. Parviz had screamed in the first chopper, suddenly convinced they were going to drop him out. That was when a doctor had looked at him, at their first fuel-stop on some military airfield. Then they'd shot him full of dope and he hadn't shouted any more.

Now all was muffled and unreal, like the turbo fans on this 747 chasing the setting sun across the Zagros mountains while Parviz's consciousness struggled to wonder what someone intended to do with him.

'I am a political prisoner,' he mouthed to himself. 'I am asking for asylum.'

The plane was late. Hours late. It was late evening before Annie could be sure that he had not emerged. She couldn't ask for Parviz Vaziree by name. That would draw attention if anyone was watching or listening. And anyway, she did not know under what name he would be travelling.

The arrivals hall was almost empty now and Annie not quite trained enough to spot the one person there who *was* watching and listening: a rotund and cheerful man with the laughing mask of a perpetual clown. He was also playing with a very long and powerful telephoto lens fitted to a motorized SLR.

Annie walked for the third time that evening to the pay-phones down the hall: 0865 for Oxford and Uncle Jasper's number, Ashley dozing with a newspaper or book in the sitting room, she thought as the ringing tone persisted. She imagined the bloody bell waking Jasper while her father found his glasses and groped his way to the telephone in the hall.

'He wasn't on the plane,' she said when he picked it

up. She could hear him backchat with his brother and knew the phone had woken the old codger.

'Sorry if it woke you,' Ashley was saying.

'So am I,' came the grumbling reply from upstairs.

'He's not here,' repeated Annie down the phone.

'He must have been on it. He was on it the other end. Young Healey rang from the embassy.'

'It means they used the back door here,' said Annie.

A short silence from the other end. 'I'm sorry you've had a wasted journey. Are you all right to drive home?'

'I've been drinking coffee for eight hours.'

'I'll wait up for you. Make you some cocoa.'

'Go to bed, Daddy.'

A handsome, chaotic girl who cares nothing for her appearance, thought the man with the SLR and the laughing face. He watched her replace the telephone and as she did so knock her overflowing handbag to the floor in a cascade of coins and keys.

Parviz had remained on the plane when the other passengers disembarked. His blond neighbour made no move, still buried in Mickey Spillane. The hostesses were taking turns in the galley to discard their *chadors*, eyes and mouths and bodies reappearing made up for their overnight in a London disco. Parviz watched one of them moving up the aisle past them, checking the empty seats and luggage lockers.

'Eyes front, buddy,' said the blond German beside him, not even looking up from his book. 'Won't do you no good thinking about what you can't have.'

Even the hostesses had gone by the time the official came on board, a bespectacled middle-aged man who examined the passports and documents Dorff handed to him.

Parviz waited till the official looked him in the face to check the passport picture. 'I'm a political prisoner,'

Parviz said, his voice barely audible. 'I'm asking for asylum.'

The Home Office official stared at him in some surprise.

'Don't mind him,' laughed Dorff. 'He's just blinking his eyes at the outside world.'

'He's an illegal immigrant in your charge,' said the official. 'That's the only way he can be held in custody.' The official looked again at Parviz. 'Do you have any luggage?'

'Not where he came from,' said Dorff.

'I'm a political prisoner,' repeated Parviz, his voice almost fading away. 'I'm asking for asylum.'

The official nodded at the window. 'Your chauffeur's waiting on the apron.'

Parviz looked through the window at his elbow at a blue flashing lamp on the roof of a van. A black van with a uniformed policeman.

'They'll take you to the hostel,' the official said to Dorff. 'All coloureds in there, I'm afraid. Illegal immigrants.'

Dorff laughed. 'And illegal immigrants are only ever coloured.' He turned to Parviz, still laughing. 'You're in the land of the free, buddy. The home of democracy!'

4

Dover's white cliffs were the colour of gunmetal as Morgan walked the ferry deck and watched gulls cry over a grey sea in another grey dawn. Homecoming was suitably low-key.

Once this had been the boat to carry the night ferry sleeping-cars – the timings were still more or less the same, the clientele very different: it was the dossers' passage these days, the backpack flotsam and jetsam with the odd fur coat or camel-hair who like Morgan had failed to find a seat on the Sunday evening planes. Thrown off the train in Dunkirk at three o'clock in the morning, kept waiting an hour, crowded and cold in the dockside station, two hours tossing on the Channel, they now plodded wearily up the wet iron gangway to the equally inhospitable rituals of British Immigration and the squalor of the Southern Region of British Rail.

Morgan's passport was given a quick once-over before he was nodded on, but Morgan guessed the man had picked him up; privilege serial number, the *A* and double zero intended to ease his way through frontier checkpoints more often than not marked him out as someone whose arrival or departure should be registered or reported.

Even so he'd hardly expected McGovern at eight o'clock in the morning on Victoria Station, peaky and sour, wincing at the machine-gun staccatos of train doors slamming shut, knocked and nudged by the commuters streaming for the Underground. He stood at the end of the boat-train platform, egg-yolk on his moustache, scowling at the foreigners shuffling past with their packs and plastic bags. After ninety minutes on a dirty, buffet-less train through whose windows it had been impossible to see, they no doubt felt like scowling back at him.

McGovern was even more seedy than Morgan remembered, his Smethwick sing-song now a positive whine. 'Give you a lift,' he stated, with a grip like a handcuff on Morgan's arm.

'You don't know where I'm going.'

'Why else would I want to give you a lift?'

A white Rover outside was blocking the taxi rank. A young man held open the back door with a nod at Morgan.

'Where to?' asked the young man once they were inside.

'Euston,' replied Morgan.

'Euston to where?' asked McGovern next to him on the back seat.

Morgan didn't answer, looking out of his window at the red London buses in their rows and trying to remember when last he'd been back.

'Want me to put a tail on you?' asked McGovern.

'Euston to Birmingham,' said Morgan.

'Very predictable, Pike.' McGovern seemed to be addressing the young man in front. 'They call him Railway Joe and he always travels by train.' McGovern turned his head to look over his glasses at Morgan: 'Whose messenger-boy are you this time?'

Morgan did not reply.

'What's happening in Birmingham, Pike?' asked McGovern.

The young man turned his head. 'Mr Veltri, sir? Request for extradition and it was initially channelled through Interpol.'

McGovern pondered that information for a few moments, picking bacon from his teeth. 'Morgan's his first name, Pike. Morgan Hunter-Brown. You should never give him space to move. He believes he has a monopoly on honesty. He cost me a man once, rushing his flat feet in where fairies fear to tread. He tries to be nice to people. Keep him moving, Pike. He doesn't belong here.'

'I have a British passport, McGovern.' Morgan looked out at the drizzle and umbrellas in Buckingham Palace Road. 'This is my home town.'

'Not in my book it isn't. And you wouldn't want to create trouble for your brother, would you.'

There were times, thought Morgan, when McGovern positively incited violence against his person.

'The little wop, Pike. Rudi Goodgardenia. Plays the clarinet and his little piccolo, snorts coke, smokes dope and sleeps with men and boys. If you want to lean on Joe here, you lean on Rudi. Joe loves his little kid brother.'

The uniformed driver glanced at Morgan in his mirror with what seemed like half an apology in his eyes.

Pike shook his head as they ground to another halt in the traffic: 'Looks like you're going to miss your train.'

'Turn the blower on, sergeant,' said McGovern. 'Show Interpol how the real cowboys live.'

The white police car, lights ablaze and siren wailing, pulled out the wrong way round a traffic island, forcing the oncoming traffic into the side of the road.

Seven minutes later Morgan was walking down the platform ramp at Euston to step onto the train as the whistles blew. A very different train from the cattle-trucks south of the river. This one was clean and silent, with windows you could see through and uniformed stewards serving breakfast to dark suits and ties. Morgan felt decidedly scruffy as he slipped into a vacant table across the gangway from the one woman in the dining-car. An elegant woman; beautiful even, thought Morgan as he glanced at her. She had dark hair with features that

22

suggested Spain, and was very meticulously buttering a triangle of toast.

'Full breakfast, sir?' the steward asked Morgan.

Morgan nodded.

'Grapefruit?'

Morgan nodded again.

'Tea or coffee, sir?'

'A bottle of red wine.'

Across the aisle the woman looked up at him in amused surprise.

5

'Another cup of tea, Uncle J?'

Jasper grunted behind his *Telegraph*, trying, Annie knew, to overhear what his brother was saying on the phone out in the hall.

Ashley walked back into the room and resumed his sparse breakfast of toast and tea.

'Any luck?' asked Annie.

'He's going to be at Winson Green prison by day but no one seems to know where he'll spend the nights.' Ashley looked up at his daughter. 'Time, I think, for you to take a note to Jesus.'

Jasper lowered his *Telegraph* to look across the table at his brother.

'It's all right, Jasper. I promise we are not conspiring subversively.'

Dear Jasper, thought Annie later as she pedalled briskly down the Banbury Road. He has to put up with an awful lot when we come south and interrupt his steady routine. It was nearly a week now since the first phone call and their sudden departure on that same day's ferry to Uig, father and daughter on what both knew would end up as separate and adverse sides of the same mission. Unequal sides, Annie might also have said, though she still wasn't sure for whom her father was working this time.

She scooted the bike to a standstill outside Jesus College and dropped the letter into the porter's lodge.

Perhaps her father *was* on his own this time if he had to ask help from the old reptile Lennox.

Annie padlocked the bike where it was and walked through Ship Street to the shops. She hadn't thought about clothes when they'd packed in such a hurry last week. If there was to be any chance of seeing Parviz she'd want something more attractive than the rag-bag of old sweaters and jeans and loose frocks she'd been wearing on the island. Not for the first time in these past few days she felt a pull at her heart, the pain and the panic she thought she'd left behind six years ago.

6

There was already a couple of newsmen in the street when Morgan arrived – one journalist and his photographer. Not all that unusual outside a prison, though Morgan filed their presence away to be remembered. Morgan did not see a third man – rotund and cheerful, with an SLR and a vast telephoto, sitting in a beige Metro fifteen yards beyond the gates and taking pictures of each person and vehicle that entered or left the prison. Morgan's was the third taxi to arrive in five minutes.

The bleakness, smells and sounds of prison closed in on Morgan as he remembered school had closed round him at the beginning of each term. The building was identical, that institutional Gothic so beloved by the Victorians. A uniformed warder dangled his keys off one finger as he showed him upstairs to the office set aside for them.

Morgan had been warned about Josef Dorff but Dorff, it seemed, had not been warned about Morgan, his mouth slowly opening as he looked up from his book and saw him walk in.

'Goddam, it's Railway Joe. Haven't they retired you yet?'

It was a secretary's ante-room Morgan found himself in; the secretary, trim and stern, glancing up at him from her typewriter then pretending not to listen as she returned to her work.

Morgan nodded at Dorff. There was a long window

in the wall behind him and people beyond it in an inner office.

Dorff was watching Morgan without enthusiasm. 'What have you been sent with, Joe?'

'Not a lot.' Morgan had picked out Veltri, dark and squat, deep in conversation with a pin-striped gentleman – presumably his lawyer. A third man was sitting at the table with his back turned to Morgan. A woman beside him glanced up at Morgan through the glass – the pretty woman from the dining-car on the train. Morgan had seen her four places ahead of him in the taxi queue at New Street Station. 'Who's the lady?'

'The interpreter,' replied Dorff. 'We've three languages here, Joe.' He handed Morgan a sheet of paper with a list of the names: Veltri's solicitor, Mr Fox; the interpreter, Mrs Colraine; the Italian *magistrato*, Mr Assuntino. Morgan looked up again through the window. Roberto Assuntino? Bob?

He turned to Dorff: 'And Mr Parviz Vaziree?'

'Squatting on the thunder-box. He's been trying to shit ever since he got off the plane last night. He blows wind like the air brakes on a truck – and me, I have to share a room with him.'

'Three years of chick-peas in his bowels,' said Morgan. 'How did you manage to extract him so easily?'

'Government signatures in Teheran. When he answers his questions he goes back where he came from.'

'I'm sure that must make him feel very useful.'

'I'm doing him a favour, Joe. He has a ride in an airplane and he gets not to eat chick-peas for a few days.'

The outside door was opened by a prison warder. Morgan stared at the pale ghost who walked in: torn sandals on bare feet caked in dirt, and a sunken face barely compatible with the photograph of the dark-suited young politician in the file.

Morgan held out his hand. 'Mr Vaziree? My name's Hunter-Brown. Interpol.' Parviz stared back at him, a moment of surprise before he responded and held out

27

his own hand. It was the first time anyone had offered to shake hands with him since the Baha'i boy had found out who he was on his first night in the camp three years ago.

The warder led Parviz into the inner room. Morgan was watching through the glass. He saw Veltri look up, recognize Parviz and freeze as though a ghost had walked in. He'd probably not even known that Parviz was still alive.

Morgan closed the connecting door and turned back to Dorff. 'Mr Vaziree needs a set of decent clothes and a pair of shoes.'

'So?'

'So draw them on expenses.'

'You mean I have to dress the bum as well?'

'He shouldn't be walking around like that if he's our responsibility. He could also do with a bath.'

Dorff stood up, exasperated. 'Whose joke was it sending you here?'

'Elgin.' Morgan pulled the red box-file out of the bag.

Dorff glaring at it. 'I thought this was my operation.'

'You know Interpol, Dorff. No one has any real authority.'

'So how come you have the red file?'

'Just for the record.' Morgan opened the door to follow the others.

Assuntino stood up as he walked in, bespectacled, fortyish, with the face of an intellectual and an occasional smile that had, not so many years ago, been very familiar to Morgan: Roberto Assuntino, one of the state prosecutors from the *procuratore*'s office in Milan. Morgan had worked with him investigating links between German and Italian terrorists. Five years ago, thought Morgan, as the two of them shook hands without public display of recognition – the instincts of caution surviving from those dangerous years. Morgan looked beyond him with a nod for the interpreter: the dark lady from Spain, if Spain it really was. That now seemed unlikely, since the languages she was translating were Italian and Persian. He wondered if she had recognized him from the train.

Her accent turned out to be purest Roedean and Oxford English. 'We are here this morning,' she said, translating from a handwritten sheet of paper that Assuntino had prepared, 'to establish common ground for an affidavit, not only to be used in our application for extradition, but to be admissible also in an Italian court of law, should Signor Veltri be brought to trial there.'

Morgan looked at Veltri. He was staring at papers on the table in front of him; both he and Parviz were avoiding eye contact. As the interpreter started her translation into Persian, Parviz looked up at her. 'I speak and understand English,' he said.

The interpreter smiled in surprise. 'Then why,' she asked, 'am I being paid for three languages?'

Her question was unanswered, the *magistrato* pointing her to the next paragraph on his sheet of notes, a question for Parviz that she put in both English and Italian. 'Can we establish that you, Mr Vaziree, first met Mr Veltri eight years ago?'

Veltri's solicitor was busy scribbling notes, the others all waiting for Parviz's reply. Instead there was a long silence. The interpreter started to phrase the question in Persian.

Parviz pushed his chair back and stood up. 'I am not here of my own free will,' he said. 'I am a political prisoner in my own country. I will not answer questions until my legal status here has been defined.'

'Your status, buddy boy,' said Dorff beside him, 'is illegal immigrant.' He grabbed Parviz's arm and pulled him back into the chair.

The interpreter was murmuring an Italian translation for Assuntino's benefit. Parviz looked across the table and caught her eye. 'I am a political prisoner,' he said in a low voice. 'I am asking for asylum.'

Mrs Colraine stared at him for a moment in silence

and surprise before translating, and this time Assuntino looked over at Morgan.

'Your legal status, Mr Vaziree, is that of illegal immigrant in custody,' said Morgan quietly. 'If you do not cooperate you will be returned to where you came from.'

'Like presto, buddy,' interrupted Dorff not so quietly. 'On the airplane this evening and back to your chicken coop.'

There was another silence, then the *magistrato* tried again, rephrasing his original question to the interpreter, who addressed it once more in English to Parviz. 'You and your political colleagues first met with Mr Veltri in 1976?' She paused then went on. 'What was the subject of the discussion you had with him?'

Parviz glanced up across the table at Veltri, the first time their eyes had actually met. It was Veltri who now spoke, in a heavily accented English. 'We talked about the politics of oil.'

'Politics?' asked Assuntino.

'How the supply of oil is controlled by seven multinational companies. We discussed ways of avoiding that control.'

A pause while the lady translated for Assuntino. 'How?' he asked.

'By using an independent dealer. I offered my own services as a broker.'

The *magistrato* prompted another question through the interpreter. She turned to Parviz: 'And did you agree to that?'

Parviz shook his head. 'Opinion in our party was divided. Some of us do not believe that the problems of our country and our people can or should be solved with outside help. Mr Veltri's motive was and remains self-interest.'

Quite a little speech to break the ice with, thought Morgan. He watched Assuntino and guessed he would now revert to his sheet of prepared questions. Sure enough the *magistrato* pushed them over to Mrs Colraine, his finger pointing at one of them.

'You were a leading member of this political party?'

'I still am.'

'This was a political party with some expectation of power?'

'Every political party has an expectation of power. It would not otherwise be a political party.'

'In the event of democratic elections, your party had a reasonable expectation of forming a government?'

'In the event of free democratic elections we still would have every expectation of forming a government.'

Assuntino pulled out another sheet of questions and step by patient step they went on. Each meeting between Veltri and Parviz or his colleagues was catalogued, the content of each meeting analysed: formal contact in Teheran; an informal meeting in Shiraz; a publicly undisclosed visit to Veltri's villa in Portofino two months after old Vaziree's assassination.

At midday, two warders brought in coffee and sandwiches, and during the half-hour adjournment Morgan walked down the corridor to check the newsmen in the street outside. A television film crew had joined them – 'asking for Parviz Vaziree,' said one of the warders who had responded to their queries at the prison gates.

Portofino was still the subject under discussion when the *magistrato* rapped on the table at 12.30 and passed another list of handwritten questions to Mrs Colraine.

'The visit to Portofino, was this an invitation?'

Parviz nodded.

'At Mr Veltri's expense?'

'Yes,' said Veltri from across the table. 'At my expense.'

'Was any agreement reached between yourselves and Mr Veltri at this meeting?'

'Intention, not agreement,' said Parviz. 'We were talking of a hypothetical situation in the event of our political party coming to power.'

31

'What was this "intention"?'

'The direct sale of crude oil to an independent company to be set up by Mr Veltri in association with a partner to be nominated by ourselves. The company in return would guarantee the purchase of items that might, for political reasons, become unavailable from certain sources abroad.'

Assuntino leant over to prompt Mrs Colraine. 'Such as armaments?' she asked.

'Nothing in particular was specified,' said Parviz.

Another murmured prompting from Assuntino to the interpreter. Mrs Colraine altered one of the questions on the sheet in front of her, then looked up again at Parviz. 'Did Mr Veltri ever give the impression that he had had experience in the buying and selling of armaments?'

Parviz glanced at Veltri and nodded.

'Did he cite examples?'

'Yes.'

'Can you name them?'

'No.'

Assuntino said in his halting English: 'You do not remember them?'

'I have no wish to incriminate other people or other countries. They are not on trial here.'

Morgan intervened. 'No one is on trial here.'

There was a silence for a moment, then Assuntino indicated another of the questions on the sheet of paper.

'Was there any financial transaction at this time between your group and Mr Veltri?'

Another, longer silence. There was a half-smile on Veltri's face as he watched Parviz and anticipated the reluctance of his reply.

'Mr Veltri made a contribution to our political fund.'

Assuntino murmured to Mrs Colraine. 'You accepted that as normal procedure?' she asked Parviz.

'Mr Veltri insisted that it was normal procedure. He

32

said that for him it was a way of life.' Parviz looked across the table at Veltri. 'He was joking about it.'

Assuntino was silent for a few moments, then he looked at his watch, pushed his chair back and stood up. 'I thank you all for your cooperation.' He leaned down to murmur to Mrs Colraine.

'Tomorrow,' she announced, 'Mr Assuntino would like the proceedings formally recorded.'

Assuntino gathered his papers, bowed to Mrs Colraine and to the others at the table. '*Grazie,* Signora Colraine. Good afternoon, gentlemen.' He walked, limping slightly, to the door.

A warder was waiting for Veltri at the door. The solicitor followed him out, with a neutral smile for anyone who caught his eye. Dorff pulled Parviz to his feet. Parviz looked round at Morgan, then across the table at Mrs Colraine. He addressed himself to Mrs Colraine. 'I am a political prisoner,' he said in a low voice. 'I am asking for asylum.'

Mrs Colraine looked up at him, not quite knowing what to say or do. She glanced at Morgan. Morgan stared down at the table.

Dorff pulled Parviz towards the door. Parviz now turned his urgent attention to Morgan. 'I am a political prisoner.'

Morgan was still staring at the table. 'I heard you the first time.'

Parviz's voice from behind him was louder and emphatic: 'I am asking for asylum.'

Morgan shut his eyes as though in pain, unaware that Mrs Colraine was watching him.

Dorff pushed Parviz out of the room. Morgan opened his eyes and saw Mrs Colraine watching him. He stood up embarrassed and followed the others through the ante-room into the corridor.

Assuntino was waiting for him at the foot of the stairs, apologizing in his quiet Italian. The press were outside, the interpreter perhaps vulnerable to their attentions, he

33

suggested. 'If you're both travelling in the same direction, perhaps you would be good enough to escort Signora Colraine.'

Morgan hadn't even thought in what direction he might be travelling, whether to stay overnight in Birmingham or return to London. He nodded to Assuntino.

'It's a pleasure to see you again,' murmured the Italian with a smile.

'It's a pleasure to see you walking again,' replied Morgan.

'Orthopaedic surgery in my country has become very specialized in the repair or replacement of kneecaps.'

7

'This is a formality,' Morgan assured Mrs Colraine as
they sat as far apart as possible on the back seat of the
taxi. 'I don't suppose there's any way a journalist could
identify you.'

'But if they did,' said Mrs Colraine, 'you'd rather I
didn't talk to them.'

'As I said, this is a formality.' And in fact they hadn't
even been noticed, the newsmen in the street too busy
chasing Parviz and Dorff in the closed police wagon.

They didn't speak again until after Coventry, face to
face over tea in the dining-car, Mrs Colraine buried in
Vogue, Morgan in his file. They'd both reached simul-
taneously for a teacake and both smiled.

'Are you a policeman?' she asked.

'In an international sort of way,' he replied.

'Interpol?'

Morgan nodded. 'Which makes me not much more
than a compiler of lists and statistics.'

'On crime?'

Morgan looked down at the file in his lap and
shrugged. 'On outlaws and refugees.'

She looked over the table at the photograph of Parviz
pinned to one of the papers. 'He looks as though he's
been in prison for a long time.'

'More concentration camp than prison, I imagine.'

'Is he really a political prisoner?'

Morgan nodded. 'If he'd done anything actually criminal he'd have been dead or mutilated a long time ago.'

'And his colleagues?'

'In hiding somewhere. Most of them got out of the country.' Morgan remembered the long lists of exiles through which he had laboriously worked all Sunday afternoon in Paris. He looked at Mrs Colraine. 'Do you know anything of the politics there?'

'A little.'

'His own survival is something of a mystery.'

She was silent for a moment, apparently immersed in *Vogue* again. Then she looked up. 'He's asking for asylum.'

Morgan nodded.

'No one takes any notice of him.'

'No.'

'Why not?'

'Because this country sells arms to his jailers.' There was an edge to his voice, and the two of them looked at each other for a brief moment with a kind of recognition.

'I shouldn't be asking questions, should I?' she said.

'It sometimes helps to be asked questions.'

'Why is Interpol involved?'

'They were asked to collate information about Mr Veltri. They also helped to arrange the temporary release of Mr Parviz Vaziree.'

'They?'

Morgan laughed. 'I'm a new boy on this.' He tapped the file. 'Trying to catch up. Figure it out.'

'Your organization seems to work very efficiently.'

'Efficiently?'

'The release of Mr Vaziree. It happened very quickly.'

Morgan laughed again. 'That sort of liaison usually takes months to set up.'

Mrs Colraine looked back again at her magazine, her eyes not focused on the pages she was turning. She looked up again at Morgan. He was watching her.

'My father was a political prisoner,' she said. 'A long time ago.'

8

Sunlight was shrinking into the eastern corner of both quads, an early evening scatter of activity around the porter's lodge as Annie and Ashley stepped in through the lodge gate.

'They dine at seven,' said Annie in a tone of voice her father knew to classify as dangerously volatile. 'In their butterfly costumes.'

'Remember we're both trying to help him, Annie.'

'For different ends and by different means.' Annie glanced at her father and his careful, brooding profile. So many people, including herself, had so often failed to recognize the steel behind that mild face. 'Are you doing this for Washington?' she asked.

The mild profile smiled. 'If I were doing anything for Washington, I wouldn't have to be dancing attendance here on a pompous, superannuated barrister.'

It was Annie's turn to smile at the venom in her father's words as they climbed the steps and passed the college hall, with a quick eyes-right at the silver and linen on the top table through the open doors.

Lennox was on the lawn in the second quad, one of four dons looking faintly ridiculous as they played boule in gowns and dinner-jackets.

'Hello, Lennox.' Ashley rather mistimed his greeting, distracting the old reptile at the moment his arm was releasing the ball.

'Bugger!' snarled Lennox and looked round. He saw Ashley and scowled further.

'Sorry to disturb, Lennox. You've had my note?'

'It's a guest night.'

Annie at the edge of the lawn listened to that pompous voice and tried not to laugh out loud.

'Have you a guest?' her father asked mildly.

'As it happens, no.' Lennox was watching one of his competitors with the ball.

'I need a bit of muscle,' said Ashley, in his ear.

'Good heavens!' Lennox seemed quite startled. 'I thought I was out of all that. I'd have thought you were, too.'

'Up to a point.' Ashley, one hand under Lennox's elbow, smiled. 'In an ideal world, wouldn't we all be cultivating our gardens?'

'I thought you were with Amnesty.'

'On and off.' Ashley had successfully detached Lennox from his game.

'Habeas corpus, Lennox. The rights of the alien.'

Annie was approaching at a tangent across the lawn.

'Alien?' Lennox didn't like the word at all.

'Don't worry,' said Annie, 'he's neither Commonwealth nor black.'

Lennox ignored her completely, still addressing himself to Ashley. 'Another victim, I take it, of man's inhumanity to man.'

'Boring isn't it,' retorted Annie, a sneer in her voice.

Lennox continued to ignore her. 'I'm meant to be teaching law, Ashley. The last thing I'm interested in is its practical application.'

'He was a pupil of yours.'

Lennox looked at him.

'Parviz Vaziree.'

Lennox pondered and looked up at the clock. 'I've no sherry in my room. Nothing to drink of any substance.'

'Just one telephone call will do.' Ashley smiled encouragingly.

'To whom?'

'He's being held as though he were an illegal immigrant. It's Home Office, Lennox. Routine police non-sense. An under-secretary will do.'

Annie watched them walk together to the staircase in the corner of the quad, contemporaries with a mutual loathing of each other, yet beholden through some ritual of establishment etiquette.

Locked in the police van, Parviz had seen the cameras in the street outside the prison and heard the voices trying to attract his face to the window. Would the outside world now be told that he was not only alive but actually out of prison, however temporary and conditional his release might be? The need to communicate with someone was painful. Perhaps if one of his own people came to know he was alive there'd be a way to make contact, if only to ask who else was still alive.

The police van had used siren and blue lamp to cross a pair of red lights and shake off the cars that tried to follow. They'd then stopped in a drab suburb, while Dorff measured him in the back of the van with a borrowed tape, but without the delicacy of the tailor in Oxford who had once made Parviz's suits.

'The man says I have to buy you clothes, Garibaldi.' A pair of jeans, a denim jacket, shirts, socks, pants and trainers: Dorff clearly resented each penny spent and practically threw the clothes at him when his reluctant shopping spree was over.

Now to add injury to insult, Dorff had had to stand outside the bathroom door in the 'hostel' while Parviz used soap and hot water on his body for the first time in three years. A bathroom with no lock on the door, bars on the window and slot machines for disposable toothbrush and plastic safety razor.

Two days ago Parviz and the Baha'i boy had shaved one another with a similar plastic razor that had by then lasted them eighteen months.

Parviz listened to the planes on the runways half a

mile away and watched the way the light was fading through the window. He knelt on the ground, head bowed to the floor in prayer towards what he hoped was the east.

9

Morgan had ridden almost in silence with Mrs Colraine in a taxi from Euston, and then with an apology continued to lurk in her garden – against the unlikely possibility that someone had followed or traced them from Winson Green.

Expensive bloody place, he thought – four or five bedrooms facing the canal in Little Venice complete with garage and garden. Either Mr Colraine was very rich or Mrs Colraine made a lot out of her interpreting. He watched her through the windows while she took off her coat and scarf and gloves and repossessed her house.

Expensive bloody furniture and all, he also thought, as he watched her move from room to room upstairs to change and back downstairs into the kitchen at the rear of the house. There was a child's swing on the lawn and thirty yards or so of flower-beds, shrubbery and lawn down to a high wall at the end of the garden – with a garden door in the wall, Morgan noticed. Not the easiest house to guard unobtrusively, and he wondered how long he ought to stay and where the hell he would then go to pass the night.

Monday evening, he thought. Where does Rudi play clarinet on a Monday evening, or has he managed to get his piccolo back into one of the orchestras? Perhaps it was more simple to find a cheap hotel, and leave Rudi and memories alone.

He heard a car pull up in the road outside and walked up the steps at the side of the house to watch the drive.

A chauffeur-driven black car and the slim-built Mr Colraine – American, Morgan realized, as he heard him say goodnight to the driver. He also heard him call to his wife as the front door opened and closed: 'Laleh!'

She was depressed without quite knowing why. As though the day had absorbed all her energy and concentration and left nothing in their place, except questions. Perhaps she simply didn't remember how tiring interpreting could be. It had been eight years since she'd last worked, apart from the odd, informal occasion at one or other of the London embassies.

Cal was predictably furious when she told him the job was not yet over. 'You've got responsibilities here,' he'd said that morning, and reminded her now of their party on Wednesday evening.

'I'll manage,' she said.

She heard his voice again from the sitting room, outrage this time coloured with alarm: 'There's a man in the garden, I'd better phone the police.' The latest exercise in embassy security had rendered them all paranoid.

'He's my personal bodyguard, Cal,' she called from the kitchen.

'Your what?'

'There were reporters outside the prison. He has to make sure I'm not got at.' Laleh walked through to the sitting room.

Cal was standing at the window. 'Looks more like a tramp than a bodyguard,' he said. 'What's the melodrama in Birmingham?'

'A political refugee.'

Cal turned away from the window. 'You might have offered your poor tramp a drink.'

With Mr Colraine back in charge of his home, Morgan reckoned his duty was done. He retrieved his bag from behind the garage and turned out of the gate and up the street: six cars parked, he counted instinctively, one of them a new arrival, the driver still in his seat. A beige Metro with a round-looking man, his face turned away as Morgan passed.

Morgan walked on round the next corner before retracing a couple of steps to look once more at the canal bank road down the line of hedges and gates. The round man had now left his car, sauntering up the street and into the Colraine's gateway. Morgan waited until he was out of sight, then walked quickly back the way he'd come in time to catch the distant sound of greetings as the round man's knock at the door was answered.

'Holy cow!' was Mr Colraine's greeting.

'Holy stranger,' the response. The round man was also American, the two men apparently old buddies.

'Well, I'm damned – come on in. Hey, Lal! Shut your eyes!'

And that was all Morgan heard before the front door closed. Enough to satisfy him that an old friend had called. Innocuous enough, though instinct prevailed again and Morgan made a mental note of the Metro's registration number.

'Shut your eyes, Lal!'

Laleh had known right away who it was. There weren't that many people in the world who could draw a playful tone out of her husband. Obediently she shut her eyes.

'Guess who?'

'Roundie.' She opened her eyes with a smile, and laughed when she saw it really was.

Roundie kissed her: 'Mrs Ambassador!'

'Not yet, Roundie.'

'Nor ever likely to be,' said Cal.

'How did you know it was me, Lal?'

'The apprehension in Cal's voice.'

Cal laughed. 'It's no use coming to me here, Roundie.

43

I couldn't even get you off a parking ticket in this town.'
Cal hovered at the drinks table.

'Me cause no trouble, sheriff!'

'Bourbon?'

'Four fingers, Cal.'

'You have to be special nice to Laleh today. She's gone back to work.'

Roundie raised round eyes above his perpetual grin. 'Back on the game? I don't believe it!'

'She's very highly paid,' said Cal as he poured drinks. 'Two-fifty a day plus travel time.'

'Where you travelling?'

'Birmingham.'

'Jesus. What happens in Birmingham?'

Cal carried over Roundie's four fingers of bourbon. 'Laleh's into heavy metal. They've even given her a bodyguard.'

Laleh frowned at her husband. 'Cal!'

'Who's "they"?' asked Roundie, raising his glass.

'I have no idea,' replied Laleh.

'A scarecrow in the garden, if he's still there,' said Cal. 'You might see him if you're sick in the flower-beds again tonight.'

'That only happened once in my life,' protested Roundie.

'Santiago,' remembered Laleh with a laugh.

'All over the British Ambassador's lupins.'

'Demasiado alegria!'

'Demasiado Jack Daniels.'

Roundie laughed; sat at the piano and ran a trill with his right hand. 'What's so important that needs your languages in Birmingham, Lal?'

Cal looked up at Roundie. 'There's no point in their giving her a bodyguard if she shoots her mouth off at the first newspaperman who walks through the door.' Cal's voice was friendly but firm.

Roundie held up both arms in surrender and laughed again.

10

London creeps back into you, thought Morgan, like Prufrock's yellow fog and the smells of a Soho evening; or Beth pushing her barrow home from Berwick Street, a tired smile and a 'hello, dearie' as though he'd never been away.

Or like Rudi's laughing face as he saw Morgan walk into the pub. Morgan sat till closing time playing pontoon with Beth, both of them raising clenched left fists when Rudi had the band play 'Maryland'.

They walked Beth home, bought Chinese fish and chips and the early editions in Fleet Street and chased each other the length of Old Compton Street like the couple of schoolboys they'd once been there, hiding their caps and school blazers as they crept off the bus to sneak back home.

Rudi had changed digs yet again, squeezed between Wardour Street and Berwick Street in a one-and-a-half-room attic above three floors of 'schoolgirl', 'rubber school-ma'am', and 'oral French'.

Morgan appraised both rooms, and Rudi's mess. And picked a very large bra from a heap of clothes on the floor. 'You been dressing up, or are you sleeping with girls these days?'

'Ringing the changes,' grinned Rudi.

Morgan summoned up the fruity tones of their one-time and unlamented housemaster: 'Dear Mr Giugiardini' – Morgan looked across the room at Rudi – 'it has come most unfortunately to my notice that your younger son has developed what I can only describe as an unnatural affection for another boy in his same dormitory.'

Rudi was waiting for it, chiming in with his brother for a family chorus: 'Loath though I am – '

They both laughed, and Rudi took the bra out of Morgan's hand. 'Don't worry, old love, she won't come tonight. She drives lorries.'

Rudi emptied the fish and chips onto a dish and Morgan opened the bottle of wine he'd been nursing in his bag all evening. 'Mamma,' he said, 'would not have considered this a suitable meal for good Italian boys.'

Rudi laid out glasses and plates. 'Perhaps things would have worked out better if she'd let us be just that.'

'Good Italian boys?'

'Instead of ersatz English.' Rudi looked at Morgan. 'British in the head.'

Morgan picked squid and garlic out of the dish. 'Do you ever wonder what might have happened if *we* had taken on the shop?'

'We could have made a go of it. The two of us together.'

'Salame and baccalà.' Morgan laughed. 'Italian grocers instead of Italian gipsies.'

Rudi poured the wine. 'You're the gipsy, old son. I'm a mere *lazzarone*.'

Morgan watched him across the table: 'Does that mean you're in trouble with someone?'

Rudi laughed. 'I wouldn't tell you if I was.' He nodded at the door. 'I don't want you on the rampage out there.'

'Nobody touches my kid brother, right?'

'Right.' Rudi grinned.

'Charles Turner-Smith and Harry Lindsay.' The two brothers chewed squid and roast duck and looked at each other. Rudi didn't rise to the bait. 'In the rackets court on a late autumn evening when you should have been at choir practice.' Morgan mimicked the fruity aristocratic voice: 'Googardini's daddy is an Italian grocer, Charles.' Morgan could remember the scene quite vividly – Rudi,

46

thirteen years old, standing against the front wall of the court while the two older boys banged the fast hard ball against the wall all round him. Then the sinister Charles as Morgan had come tiptoeing into the gallery: 'Drop your trousers, Googie. Let's see your tiny tool.'

'Let's see your tiny tool,' Morgan said out loud and Rudi laughed again.

'You fucking nearly killed them.'

Morgan raised his glass. 'Blood thicker even than wine, Rudi.'

'Latin blood,' corrected Rudi. 'Anglo-Saxon body fluids run like spilt tea in the rain.' He filled up his brother's glass. 'Does anyone know you're in town?'

Morgan nodded.

'McGovern?'

Morgan nodded again. 'If you have junk in the flat you'd better get rid of it.'

'I've been clean for months. Anyway, I can't afford it.' Rudi was watching Morgan. 'Your smile's looking tired, Joe. Something's changed in you.'

'Old age, little brother. It must be ten years since I've been allowed to do anything I actually believe in.' He looked down at the pile of newspapers they'd carried from Fleet Street, then looked up at Rudi.

Rudi held up a hand to stop him. 'Don't tell me anything. I don't want to know. If they start pulling out my finger-nails I'd tell tales even on you.'

Morgan found it in the *Guardian* two hours later when Rudi was asleep. 'PRISONER OF CONSCIENCE TESTIFIES IN WINSON GREEN – on the back page with a photograph of Parviz. More black ink-smudge than photograph; Morgan wondered why the old *Grauniad* even bothered to print pictures.

11

Annie surveyed the room. Her two hours' work since daybreak had made little impression. It still looked like Uncle J's boxroom, full of family *memorabilia* that no one had quite had the heart to throw away. She leant from the open window to pick two red roses from the rambling climber on the wall outside and stuck them in a jar on the bedside table.

She heard the newspapers being pushed through the door downstairs, the boy's bicycle on the road and her father's step on the stairs. Sweep the floor first or strip the bed, she wondered, pushing one old trunk into a corner.

There was another creak on the stairs and her father pushed open the door, a newspaper in his dressing-gown pocket.

'Sorry, Daddy,' said Annie. 'Did I wake you up?'

Ashley closed the door behind him. 'Try not to thump around too much. Don't want to disturb Jasper. I think he will already not be best pleased with how we intend to use the house.' Ashley watched his daughter strip the bed, years of dust rising in clouds. 'Where will the other one sleep?'

'In the garage, for all I care.'

'He has to be with Parviz. That is one of the conditions.'

'Sod the conditions.'

'We cannot afford to, Annie. He's allowed to come

here for one night and talk – in the company of his escort. And leave with his escort next morning.'

'Scout's honour, is it?' Annie sneered. 'Given our word to someone, have we? I seem to recall you giving your word to his father six years ago.'

Ashley pulled out the *Guardian* and laid it on the bed, folded to Parviz's picture and the back-page headline. Annie looked at it in surprise.

'Two cheers for British journalism,' she said.

'I doubt it, Annie. That feels more like a careful and deliberate leak from somewhere.'

'At least people will know he's alive.'

'And know *where* he is.'

'Well?'

'I wonder who was meant to read this.' Ashley withdrew, closing the door quietly behind him.

Annie stared at the smudged photograph. She felt that pull at her heart again. The pain and the panic. She decided the red roses looked silly, but left them where they were.

12

Morgan saw him the moment he turned into the street a hundred yards or more from the prison – six foot six, barrel-chested, bearded, scruffy and apprehensive, eventually propping up a wall and trying without success to look inconspicuous.

Morgan had arrived early, not quite knowing why but anticipating something. The *Guardian* and *Morning Star* were carrying Parviz's picture and, as he later found out, Channel Four had run the Parviz story as a brief item on their news the evening before.

The bearded giant made his move as soon as he saw the police van approach through the traffic. He headed the van off like a tank on deliberate collision course. Morgan caught up with it as it halted at the prison gates, running to intercept him, suddenly convinced that the bearded giant was carrying a gun or a grenade.

Instead, the man suddenly stopped short only to look and stare. Parviz, inside the van, had seen him, pressing his face against the bars of the window. Bearded man and Parviz gazed at each other in startled recognition for one brief moment before the van moved on through the gate.

Behind them along the street, Morgan heard a car start up – a beige Metro that moved quickly past him, the registration number familiar to Morgan, as was the shape of the rotund man behind the wheel. This time Morgan saw his face and noticed an SLR camera with a large zoom lens on the front seat beside him. Morgan looked round, but the bearded man had vanished. The street had resumed its normal pattern.

Morgan might have asked himself later whether anything had really happened out there. But it was enough to see Parviz's face in the room upstairs to know that his sight of the bearded man had had a profound effect on him.

Morgan picked out the bearded face from one of the photographs in the file: Farshid Sabet, dressed formally for some political occasion seven or eight years ago. The party intellectual.

'He used to write their pamphlets and policy documents,' said Dorff. 'Still does. Telephones a satirical column into an underground newspaper once a week. No one knows where from.' Dorff had also done his homework. 'If he *was* out in the street you should have tailed him, Joe. There's a lot of people like to know where Farshid Sabet hides.'

'We are not a political organization.'

'Of course not, Joe.' Dorff laughed. 'We tail everyone impartially, left or right, black or white.'

Farshid might have claimed he was neither black nor white, neither right nor left – but then he also had no idea he was being tailed: on the bus to New Street Station; on the train to Oxford; on another bus that meandered over the Berkshire Downs; and finally three miles on foot along a country lane to the derelict caravan where he lived on the edge of a farmyard, and in time to round up the farmer's cows for four o'clock milking.

13

An official stenographer was called to the prison that afternoon to record a statement from Parviz – the replies to the *magistrato*'s questions drawn out of him the previous day and repeated in the morning session. Since it was to be a legal document admissible under both English and Italian law, the preamble was conventionally formal.

'Name?' asked the stenographer, looking up at Parviz.

'Parviz Vaziree.'

'Domicile?'

Parviz looked at her for a moment. 'I am a political detainee, imprisoned without trial, somewhere in the Dasht-e-Kavir.'

The stenographer looked at the *magistrato*; the *magistrato* looked at Veltri's English lawyer.

'No fixed abode?' suggested the lawyer.

The stenographer tapped it out and looked up again at Parviz: 'Date of birth?'

'Fourth of April, 1944.'

'Occupation?'

Again a moment's pause before he answered: 'Democrat.' The word was spoken with a certain defiance.

Morgan saw Mrs Colraine turn her head away with a sudden look of pain, almost tears in her eyes, he thought.

Later, playing the role of bodyguard again, Morgan watched her on the train. She stared out at lines of trees and hedges, her mind a thousand miles away, or so it seemed. She looked round once, embarrassed when she saw him watching.

'Where did your Italian come from?' he asked.

'I was born in Italy,' she replied. 'By chance. My father was a refugee from Spain.'

So, Morgan had been right about the Spanish. He was still watching her; she was looking at him.

'They told us there was an amnesty. He was killed by Franco's police when he tried to take us home. I was six years old.'

'Is that what you were thinking of today? You seemed upset.'

'My mother told me he always used to describe himself as a democrat. He wanted that written on his grave. It was strange to hear that man today using the same word in that same way.'

'And was it written on his grave?'

She shook her head. 'We never knew where he was buried. We had to run away.' She turned her head to the window again and Morgan refrained from any more questions.

He was middle-aged, wore round metal-frame glasses and was sitting on the wall smoking a pipe. A broken white wall somewhere in Andalucía. She could conjure up each blade of grass in the hillside behind him, just by glancing across the room at him. He had, she realized, been sitting in that silver frame, untouched for twenty years. And she, on that hot dry hillside had, he'd told her, 'come home.'

'Are you ready, Lal?' Cal called from the next room. She could see Cal through the mirror, tying his bow-tie, his movements precise and fastidious. She looked away, turning on her dressing-table lamp.

'We'll be late.' Cal walked into the bedroom, hunting through his drawer for a handkerchief to match his cummerbund. 'Shall I choose something for you to wear?'

'Would you mind frightfully if I didn't come?'

53

Cal looked round in surprise. 'I wouldn't mind frightfully, but I'm sure the Italian Ambassador will mind very frightfully. He wants to hear all about Veltri.'

'Well, I couldn't tell him anyway, could I?'

'You have diplomatic immunity, darling.' Cal crossed the room to stand behind her, hands on her shoulders. 'Come and glitter for me, Lal.'

She reached for a brush to move away from his touch. 'Why? Have we been told to be particularly nice to the Italians?'

'We're always nice to all our NATO allies. Especially those who give us missile room.'

'I wish – ' she said, and left it unfinished.

'The food'll be good.'

'I wish we didn't always have to play games.'

'But you like the Italians.'

'I mean the being careful. The pretending.'

'You're very good at it, Lal.' His voice was cold suddenly. 'It seems to come naturally enough to you.'

Morgan watched him leave: overcoat on one arm, silk scarf, gloves and a waiting chauffeur. A man of substance.

The limousine purred away up the canal bank, its tail-lights red in the dusk. Morgan decided to wait for darkness. He'd had his chance to leave half an hour ago when Mr Colraine returned home, and had only lingered for the coincidence of that beige Metro outside the prison that morning.

He was sitting on the child's swing in the back garden when she called him.

'It's cold out there,' she said. 'If all you're doing is protecting me from the media, you can do that just as well indoors.' She was standing at the top of the iron steps that led up from the garden to the kitchen door.

'It's all beer and whisky in this house, I'm afraid,' she said as he walked in. She'd changed into a pair of slacks and a sweater. 'And when there is wine, it's always Californian.'

'Your husband's American?'

'Diplomatic booze. He works at the embassy.'

'Whisky's fine.'

He watched her through an open arch at the drinks table in the sitting room. It seemed they were to stay in the kitchen.

'No hawkers, no circulars,' he said as she returned.

She looked puzzled.

'When I was a boy, this sort of house would have had little brass plates on the gate to keep gipsies and tradespeople away.'

'You lived in "this sort of house"?'

Morgan laughed. 'Good Lord, no.' He topped up his whisky with water from the tap. 'I lived over the family shop in Soho. School was in "this sort of house", until we were thirteen.'

She smiled. 'Prep school.'

'Brown blazers and grey flannel shorts and God help you if you stuttered or didn't play games or had a funny name.'

They sat down across the kitchen table in the fading light. 'What was *your* funny name?' she asked.

'Guiseppe Giugiardini.'

'You're Italian?'

Morgan smiled. 'It all gets obscured, doesn't it?'

'Do you still live in London?'

'My brother does.'

'Where is your home?'

Morgan held up his bag. 'Here. Hotel rooms and left-luggage lockers on railway stations.'

'You sound like one of your outlaws or refugees.'

'I expect that's why I'm meant to understand them so well.'

She stood up and opened the fridge, the light from the inside suddenly bright on her face. 'I was once a refugee.' She returned to the table with a can of beer and gesturing with one hand above the table. 'When I was so high. We were DPs. Do you remember DPs?'

'Displaced persons.'

She poured the beer and sipped at it. 'My father was in hiding.' She was silent for a moment. 'I thought I'd forgotten about all of that long ago.'

Morgan watched her. 'Your father was killed, you said.'

Laleh stared at the table. 'They came for him one night. I watched them. He hadn't done anything wrong and they didn't know what to do with him. So they started tearing up the books in his room and he lost his temper and attacked them. Then they were able to shoot him.' She looked up at Morgan. 'My mother was Persian. We never had the right papers to cross the frontiers.'

The kitchen was almost dark. Morgan would have liked to touch her hand on the table. 'Do you have children?' he asked eventually.

'Two boys. At boarding school.' She laughed. 'Yes – God help them if *they* ever stutter or don't play games. I'm afraid I went to the same sort of place. Brown blazers and grey flannel skirts. England is where we finished up. I mean me and my mother.'

'England has never been a notoriously easy place to get into if you don't have money or the right papers.'

'My mother married an Englishman. For security. For the passport.' She looked at Morgan. 'As I married my husband. I have two passports.' She laughed quickly to change the subject. 'You weren't on the train this morning. No bottles of wine on the breakfast table.'

Morgan smiled. 'There was a bottle, on an earlier train.'

'You went up early to watch the street outside the prison?'

Morgan nodded.

'Because of what was in the papers?'

'Well guessed,' said Morgan, surprised at her intuition.

56

'It was as good as a signpost, wasn't it?'

'Whose signpost?'

Laleh shrugged. 'And was anyone there?'

Morgan nodded. 'I think so.'

'Is that a good thing or a bad thing?'

'From whose point of view?'

'I don't know,' replied Laleh. 'Whose side are we meant to be on?'

'An interpreter isn't meant to be on anyone's side.'

'Whose side are *you* on?' she asked.

'I suppose, like your father, I would settle for the same epitaph on my gravestone: "Democrat". But then doing the job I do, I would not have earned it, would I.'

Morgan finished his drink and stood up. 'On hotel registers in France guests used to have to write their occupation and their destination. The poet Shelley used to declare his occupation as Democrat; his destination as Hell.'

There was a board by the kitchen phone. Morgan scribbled an address and a telephone number. 'My brother's number,' he said. 'Just in case.'

Laleh laughed. 'You sound like the security people at the embassy.'

'Thank you for the drink, Mrs Colraine.'

Laleh led him down the hall to the front door. Morgan faced her as she opened it: 'Did you have a visitor last night?'

'Last night?'

'Did anyone call?'

'An old friend looked in. We hadn't seen him for years. We all got a little drunk together.' Morgan was still watching her. 'Ralph Curtiss. He's a journalist.' She smiled. 'Don't worry. I didn't tell him anything.'

She watched him to the gate before closing the door; and watched again from the dark sitting room as he crossed the road to walk under the street lamps along the canal towards the buses in Edgware Road. She wished he hadn't gone; and shivered as she closed the curtains.

14

He was folded into the caravan like an outsize cuddly toy, dwarfing the table where he worked, the candle in front of him reflecting through the window in the puddles across the farmyard. The dog was barking in the shed and he looked up for a moment from his pen and paper, staring out at the darkness.

Parviz was frightened for Farshid. Careful though Farshid must have been to stay alive so long, that lovable bear of a man was far too conspicuous and emotional to be entirely safe. However far he'd had to travel that morning there'd be plenty who would have noticed him, and someone among that plenty who might have recognized him.

At least there was no sign of him when the police van left the prison that afternoon.

Their own departure had been delayed. Parviz had had the impression of muttered disbelieving phone calls in the next room – Dorff arguing with someone in his Germanic English. A pity the interpreter had gone. Parviz almost felt he trusted her.

When they did finally leave, it was only as far as a lay-by on the outskirts of the city, where another vehicle was waiting for them – an unmarked CID car complete with plain-clothes man and driver. In the comfort of the back seat Parviz eventually fell asleep.

And seemed to be dreaming still when he woke up.

There weren't many cities in the world whose outskirts he could so immediately recognize, but this was one: elderly bicycles with straw baskets ridden by girls and ageing dons; the generous avenue running north with its brother out of town, crossed by cosy side-roads and lined with gothic houses; the parade of shops in Summertown. The Banbury Road, thought Parviz. What the hell am I doing in Oxford?

Dorff looked round: 'You sleep in a different bed tonight, buddy. Seems you have British friends in high British places.'

They'd turned down one of those cosy side-roads and stopped in front of an overgrown gate and overgrown garden, with a battered yellow car parked in the long grass and a peeling gothic house behind.

Annie heard the car pull up and abandoned her preparations in the kitchen to run into the sitting room. I have to see him before he sees me, she thought, or I'll make a fool of myself in some way. Jasper was nodding, half asleep in an armchair, a book slipping from his lap. He looked up in some alarm at Annie's distraught entrance.

The plain-clothes man and driver were piling out of the front seats, in a conspicuous and self-conscious display of vigilance and deterrence. Then Annie saw the pale, thin but still familiar face and body climb out from the back of the car, looking up puzzled at the house until he saw Ashley appear at the open front door, and his expression changed to joyous disbelief.

Annie became suddenly aware of her own appearance, both hands trying to discover the state of her wild hair, brushing and smoothing at her crumpled blouse as though the creases might magically disappear. Jasper was staring at her in amazement over his reading glasses. She heard her father's voice from outside.

'We are very happy to welcome you as our guest.'

Annie walked into the hall as Ashley ushered Parviz through the door, she and Parviz staring at each other for a moment in silence. '*Khasteh nabashi*,' said Annie in greeting.

'*Kheli*,' replied Parviz. She walked forward to take his hand and lead him into the sitting room.

'Uncle Jasper, this is Parviz,' Annie called out as they entered.

'Who?' grunted Jasper, staring at Parviz. 'What's going on? Nobody tells me anything.' Poor Jasper looked even more confused as Dorff appeared in the doorway.

'You must be very tired,' said Annie to Parviz. He did look oh so exhausted, the joy of that first disbelief now becoming more guarded.

'How did you know I was here?' he asked. 'How does anyone know I am here?'

Ashley smiled at him. 'We will talk later. First you must rest, and then eat. We have tried to find a fatted calf to kill.'

Jasper grunted again in his chair.

It was late evening before they did manage to talk alone, Parviz in the bedroom Annie had prepared, Dorff on a camp-bed outside the door, Annie and Ashley saying goodnight to Parviz inside. Ashley had brought with him a small cassette player; the Mozart was just loud enough to keep their conversation private.

'There is a future for you,' Ashley had been saying in general terms over dinner. 'A future that is not wholly incompatible with all aspects of the present regime. It is the way of religious revolutions to cool and consolidate.'

'Farshid was outside the prison today,' said Parviz, as soon as the bedroom door had closed. 'He should not have come.'

Ashley shook his head. 'No.'

'They have kept me alive for three years,' said Parviz. 'Why? Why me, when all the others were killed?'

'Not all,' said Ashley. 'A few of those who fled the country are still alive. A focus for resistance.'

60

'Who of *us* is still alive?' asked Parviz. He meant the old inner council of the party.

Ashley turned up the volume of the music. 'Sasan, Shaheenee and Farshid.'

'And Sirus?'

'Sirus is dead.'

Parviz closed his eyes.

'All is not so lost as must appear to you,' said Ashley. 'If we can make contact with Sasan, Farshid and Shaheenee, the four of you would be recognized by your own supporters and by the outside world as constituting the authority of your party.' Ashley paused. 'I think the time is right to talk to the Americans.'

Annie turned to stare at her father.

'They weren't much help last time,' said Parviz bitterly.

'They found very quickly that they'd backed the wrong horse.' Ashley chose his words with care. 'Nothing is going to change in your country, Parviz, without some help from outside.'

'That is not what my father believed. Nor what he died for.'

Ashley watched Parviz for a moment, then picked up the cassette player and walked to the door. 'Perhaps in the morning you will let me know how you feel.'

Parviz and Annie watched him go, then Parviz turned to Annie. 'The Americans?'

'*I* didn't say that.'

'Who would *you* say?'

Annie walked slowly to the door.

'Whom does one trust?' asked Parviz when she faced him again, and she winced at his question as though it hurt her.

'You used to drink water in the night,' she said. 'I will bring you some.'

15

The candle was still burning in the window but the caravan was empty. Farshid, a mile away along the lane, was walking down the hill in the darkness towards the distant light of the phone-box.

As earlier, when he had heard the dog bark in the barn and felt it strange, so now he heard the sound of a car somewhere back along the lane, and also thought it unusual for midnight. Then the engine cut out and he imagined a young couple parked in one of the gateways. He hoped he wouldn't disturb them on his way home.

He pulled open the door of the phone-box, laid out three sheets of hand-written Farsi and took from his other pocket a bag of 10p pieces. Thirteen digits he dialled.

Behind him on the hill a car with no lights was freewheeling down towards the isolated glow of the phone-box.

Annie climbed the stairs with a glass of water. Dorff looked up at her from the camp-bed when she stopped in front of him. She was in a nightdress, her hair combed out, and she waited pointedly until, reluctantly, he rolled off the bed and pulled it clear of the door.

The bedroom light was off. Parviz's face on the pillow grew out of the darkness as Annie's eyes adjusted. She set the glass down by the two red roses on the bedside table and looked at him.

'It is three years,' he said, 'since I touched a woman.'

Annie pulled the nightdress over her head to stand naked in front of him.

'You frighten me,' he whispered.

Farshid was dictating from his sheets of paper, pausing every few seconds to push in coins, the telephone-box a pool of light in the darkness. The car, unseen, free-wheeled down the hill towards him. The moment Farshid finished his call and hung up, the car ran onto the grass verge behind him, nose against the kiosk door, trapping him inside. As he turned to push at the door, the car's headlights came on, blinding him. Farshid peered out, trying to shield his eyes, uncertain whether he was in danger or merely the butt of someone's late-night fun.

Then he saw the shape of a man behind the headlights climbing out of the passenger seat – an Arab with blazing dark eyes and a moustache, a gun held up two-handed to gesture Farshid away from the telephone.

The car started up and backed away from the door. The Arab slipped into the kiosk with Farshid. One blow to his middle winded him, one arm forced his head back against the glass behind him. The driver was out of the car now, a thin container in his hand. He drew out a hypodermic and exchanged it for the gun with the killer inside. Farshid's head was still jammed back against the glass, the killer holding it motionless with his arm as he slid the hypodermic up Farshid's nose.

He jabbed it high into the nasal cavity between the eyes, pushing hard with the heel of his hand until it was empty. Then he took small plugs of wax and cotton from his pocket, forcing them with a wooden toothpick up both nostrils until the bleeding was staunched. He cleaned nose and nostrils, still holding Farshid's head back against the glass; and waited until Farshid's knees gave way to let the body slide down and fold up on the floor.

Farshid's eyes continued to watch the killer as he walked back to the car. Another twenty minutes were to pass before his head rolled slowly sideways against the glass.

PART TWO

'Noughts and Crosses'

1

Annie ran her hand down the line of Parviz's face in the darkness. She would have liked to touch his body again with her hand and with her mouth but sensed that his inability to respond humiliated him. 'You once wrote to me,' she whispered, '"the age of a tree is measured by rings in the wood, the age of a man by the sum of his despair".'

'We have a few hours of one night,' he replied with a bitter laugh. 'That is for the moment enough despair.'

Perhaps she hadn't been very skilful at hiding her disappointment. Of all her few lovers, the physical joys shared with Parviz had always been the most complete. Unwisely she had allowed herself to anticipate them, just as now she began to anticipate the pain of his departure in the morning.

He told her instead of the Baha'i boy who at times for warmth or comfort shared his chicken-wire bed in the darkness of the prison night; told her what the boy had taught him of the fundamentals of his gentle and much persecuted religion; whispered to her the Arab poem the boy had been so fond of reciting:

Early evening over a neglected village
And two eyes dreaming.
I go back thirty years and five wars.
I see that time holds for me a grain of hope.
The Singer sings about fire and strangers.

And the evening was evening
And the Singer was singing . . .

It was dawn before Parviz slept and Annie slipped away.

2

The farmer heard the cows at half past seven, loud in protest at the yard gate. In the caravan there was no sign of life, but the candle burnt out in its saucer.

'Bugger's drunk down at the pub more'n likely,' he grumbled to his wife, and sent her off in the old van to look for him while he did the bloody milking himself.

Find him she did, one and a half miles down the lane. She saw him by chance, his head just visible against the lowest line of glass in the kiosk, her old van braking and snaking on the loose gravel as she stopped to back up. Must be drunk as a skunk to sleep it off in a phone-box.

'Bless me, young man, what are you doing?' she said as she opened the door. Then touched his arm and hand and found him stone-cold.

Parviz raised the bedroom window onto a North Oxford morning, soft with sunshine and smell and shrill prep school sounds across the road, where boys were arriving in clusters out of mothers' cars.

The CID man was standing on the rough back lawn looking up at him, walkie-talkie in hand, watching with careful attention as Parviz picked a red rose from the climber on the wall by the window.

Dorff frowned at the rose outside the bedroom door, Ashley smiled at it as he met Parviz down in the hall. 'Breath of fresh air?' he asked, and led Parviz across the dining room through the French window, leaving Dorff to face Jasper's glare over the lowered *Telegraph* across the breakfast table.

Ashley picked a way into the long grass. The CID man retreated to the far corner of the garden wall. Someone, thought Parviz, must have been very specific about leaving them to talk alone.

'There were flower-beds somewhere here when my mother was alive,' said Ashley, peering into the grass. 'It's all very sad. My dear brother Jasper is no gardener, I'm afraid.' He turned to look at Parviz. 'Your father was a botanist, I believe, before he became – '

' – an unsuccessful politician.'

'Hardly unsuccessful.'

'He was assassinated. That's a form of failure.'

'You never discovered . . . ?'

'My father was killed because he refused to make agreements with anyone on the outside.' Parviz's voice, though low, was cold and clear. 'Whether he was murdered by the Americans or the Russians or the oil companies is no longer relevant.'

'His death made the people very angry.'

'That may have been its second purpose. Unfortunately, the control of that anger passed into the hands of people with whom my father would have had no sympathy.'

They both stepped over the rotting remains of a tennis net, still hung between its posts in the grass.

'Your father was very generous with his sympathy,' said Ashley, 'where and when he chose to give it.'

'He would not have chosen to offer it to America.'

The two of them had stopped, facing each other. Ashley offered his mild and careful smile: 'What harm would it do to talk to someone from Washington before you return home?'

'Home?' Parviz laughed. 'My home, Ashley, is a wooden hut in the desert, too hot by day, too cold by night, where the guards make sport with people's mental and physical weaknesses in the name of Islam. By all the laws of logic, I should have been dead three years ago.'

'Even *they* might find it embarrassing if you were to die in one of their own prisons. "World opinion" still counts for something, however vague and undefined.'

'Then perhaps they have released me now to kill me here?'

Ashley looked shocked; pained, almost. 'My dear boy – I think you are well looked after.' Ashley offered another mild and apologetic smile. 'The more so perhaps if you were to open a dialogue.'

Parviz shook his head. 'They used to say there was no one anywhere in the world who knew more about our country than you. But you are no longer part of an embassy or a government.'

'No.'

'You must represent someone to have gone to all this trouble on my behalf.'

'I do what I am doing out of my love for your country and your culture – as once it was. And in memory of your father.'

Parviz shook his head with a smile. 'My father used to call you the English fox. I never understood whether he meant it as a term of abuse or of respect.'

Parviz heard bicycle bells beyond the garden wall and remembered girls with books in straw baskets on their handlebars. Then Annie called them in to breakfast.

3

Morgan had had a premonition all morning, a dozen newspapers from a half a dozen countries all carrying Parviz's photograph – 'like an invitation,' he'd told Laleh on the train that morning.

An invitation to death, it seemed.

The village constable had contacted Special Branch over the radio in his panda car at 08.05. The ambulancemen had found gun and papers on the body in the telephone-box. An Iranian passport, whose visitor's permit had expired eighteen months ago, and a newspaper article from yesterday's *Guardian* – 'PRISONER OF CONSCIENCE TESTIFIES IN WINSON GREEN'.

Special Branch arrived in Birmingham at midday, blue lights flashing, one hundred and ten miles in one hour up the motorway and down Lodge Road to interrupt day three of Assuntino's interrogation. McGovern was arrogant and blustering, as though he feared someone would challenge his authority.

'Looks like a meeting of the five families, Joe.' McGovern glared over his spectacles at the seven of them round the table. 'Who are the cops here and who the robbers?' He fixed on Veltri. 'Mr Vaziree?'

Morgan pointed him in the right direction and McGovern pulled a photograph from his pocket and placed it on the table in front of Parviz – a picture of Farshid as the police photographer had found him, face smudged up against the glass of the telephone-kiosk. 'Can you identify this man?'

Parviz was shown Farshid's body in a hospital morgue, labelled, already post-mortemed, the skull shaved to the ears and bandaged together where the pathologist's saw had cut.

McGovern and a local CID man were closeted in the hospital office. Morgan, not invited to hear the autopsy, and Laleh were the only witnesses to the pain on Parviz's face as Dorff walked him back to the police van in the hospital yard.

'Died some time between eleven o'clock and one last night,' Morgan told Laleh.

'Twelve hours after he'd been seen in the street outside the prison.'

'Natural causes,' said McGovern with some relief in his voice, as he climbed back into the car.

'Ventricular fibrilation due to vagal inhibition', was the official verdict typed out on the death certificate.

All the same, McGovern had requested a re-run at the telephone-box on that lonely country lane, with the farmer's wife and the local constable demonstrating the position of the body when it was found.

Parviz climbed down from the back of the police van, Dorff's arm outstretched to stop him.

'He was my friend,' said Parviz. 'I should like to see how he died.'

'Didn't know he was dead, not till I touched him,' they heard the farmer's wife say. 'Thought he was drunk.'

Morgan was watching McGovern. His questions had been very perfunctory. He'd made up his mind after the pathologist's report and was no longer interested in the other circumstances that may or may not have been relevant to the death.

Morgan smiled at the farmer's wife. She was a willing witness, if a little apprehensive somewhere behind her down-to-earth acceptance of this sudden drama in her life.

'Can you remember if the phone was off the hook?' Morgan asked her.

'Didn't look at the phone.'

'You must have used the phone to call the police.'

'Can't remember whether it was hanging down nor where it was.'

'The door was shut tight, was it?'

McGovern interrupted. 'He dropped down dead, Joe. The autopsy's done. There's nothing more to look for.'

'The door *was* shut,' said the farmer's wife. 'There was a funny smell when I opened it.'

'He'd soiled himself,' said the village bobby.

'Didn't exactly drop down dead if he had time to do that.'

'Bowels open at the moment of death. It happens sometimes.' McGovern turned back to the car. 'Interpol satisfied?'

'It's you that has to be satisfied, McGovern.'

'We've been called in for identification. An illegal immigrant carrying a gun. Routine procedure against terrorism.'

A pair of wheel marks a couple of feet from the kiosk door, almost obliterated by the day's footprints; a 10p piece among the sweet papers on the floor. Morgan tried the door. It yielded easily against the sprung arm. Morgan couldn't understand why, when that giant of a man collapsed, the door had not been forced open. He seemed to have slumped down very neat and tidy. Morgan turned back to the car, aware of Parviz watching him from the back of the van.

The caravan was far from neat and tidy – a jumble of papers and books and the paraphernalia of a single and very frugal life. It was parked, wheel-less and derelict, on one side of the muddy farmyard. McGovern collected himself a shoeful of mud and water as he briskly led the way, waving at Pike and Morgan to stay with Laleh in the car. Morgan ignored him, following him up the steps into the caravan.

McGovern picked up handwritten pages from the table, all in Arabic or Farsi. 'Get the interpreter,' he said over his shoulder at Morgan. But Morgan again ignored him, sitting on the bunk while McGovern stomped away to make his polite request to Mrs Colraine.

Morgan looked round at each detail of the dead man's life – a small gas-cylinder and ring; an old kettle and saucepan; a paraffin lamp; a shelf of tinned food; a few obviously treasured books laid out carefully above the table; a less tidy heap of newspapers and magazines on the floor; a pair of muddy wellingtons by the door. A photograph on the wall Morgan recognized from the file as Parviz's father, old Vaziree.

McGovern returned with Mrs Colraine. Morgan made room for her on the bunk, but she remained standing. McGovern hunted through papers on the desk, to pick one apparently at random and hand to her. She was a little wary of him. Like Morgan, she was looking round at the drab details of the dead man's life – an exile's hiding-place.

'Can you read it?' asked McGovern, nodding at the sheet of paper in her hand.

'It seems to be an article for a newspaper.'

'What sort of article?'

'A satirical article.'

McGovern sniffed. 'Subversive.'

'Whatever the hell that means,' said Morgan.

'It means political, Joe.' McGovern upended a box of letters on the bunk, picked out one again at random and handed it to Laleh.

She glanced at it and handed it back. 'It's a private letter. It's personal.'

'It's all part of his identity,' replied McGovern.

'You know who he is. What more do you want?'

'If he's a subversive working out of this country, I want to know everything there is to know about him.'

'He's nothing any more,' said Laleh. 'He's dead.'

McGovern dropped the letter back on the bed and looked at Morgan. 'Perhaps your prisoner would like to see where his old friend was living.'

'He's not a prisoner,' replied Morgan, but left the caravan and picked his way through the puddles to the rear door of the police van. It was locked. Parviz stared out at him through bars and rain-spattered glass. They watched each other for a moment, then Morgan turned aside to the farmhouse, ducking in out of the rain under the low back door.

Dorff, Pike, the local bobby and the CID man were sitting round the kitchen table with the farmer and his wife, mugs of tea in front of them all, laughing at a joke, then silent as Morgan walked in. He stood for a moment in the door, wiping rain off his face, then nodded at Dorff.

'Let your monkey out of that cage.'

'Catching cold is he, Joe?'

'Special Branch needs him.'

Dorff pushed past him to the back door. The farmer's wife held up the teapot.

'Cup of tea, dear?'

'I'd love one.' Morgan nodded and sat down in Dorff's place at the table. There was silence for a moment, as he looked round at them. He singled out the local bobby. 'Anyone come out with you to the body this morning?'

'Doctor from the village.'

'He took the body away, did he?'

'Ambulance came for the body.'

A mug of tea was passed down the table to Morgan and he nodded his thanks at the farmer's wife. 'Been with you long, had he?' Morgan saw the farmer look up as his wife answered.

'He came eighteen months ago.'

'Working for you?'

76

The farmer replied, sharp-faced and sharp-voiced. 'No. Not work. He had the caravan and did the milking for it. I never paid him no wages.'

That's their apprehension, thought Morgan. A cow-hand on the cheap, paying neither stamps nor tax. Morgan turned to the local bobby. 'You never had to write a report on him?'

'No call, was there?' He was also a shade guarded. 'I didn't know he didn't have his papers. Behaved himself in the village. Got drunk a couple of times. Landlord looked after that. Poached the odd pheasant with a stone, they said, but I never saw him.'

'Stone?' asked Pike.

'He'd take bets,' said the farmer's wife. 'Toss a stone in the air and he'd hit it with another stone.'

The policeman nodded: 'Way he went hunting as a kid,' he said.'

Morgan looked back at the farmer. 'Did he ever get letters?'

'Not here, he didn't. Went somewhere else for them.'

'London?'

'Not my business to ask.'

Silence again as Morgan finished his tea. He stood up with a nod for Pike. 'Your boss was quick off the mark this morning.'

Morgan stood for a moment at the back door, staring out at the drizzle. He could see Dorff sheltering under the tarpaulin to one side of the caravan. Parviz was presumably inside; his turn now to contemplate the meagre life-style of his exiled companion.

McGovern was pushing letters at Parviz when Morgan rejoined them. Parviz was as reluctant as Laleh had been to say anything about them.

'They're from his wife,' he said eventually, and held up a sheet with a child's drawing on it. 'And his children.'

'Where do they live?'

'Back home.' Parviz looked up at McGovern. 'Where the streets are full of police, official and otherwise.'

'What does the letter say?'

'His wife asks him for money. His children ask him to come home and see them.' He handed back the letter. 'They, of course, are not permitted to leave their home.'

Morgan resumed his place on the bunk as McGovern turned back to the jumble of letters. He picked out a photograph – five men, Parviz and Farshid among them, and a girl, all of them grouped round old Vaziree under a large two-bladed fan in what looked like an airport lounge. 'Is that all of you?' he asked Parviz.

Parviz did not reply. Another car had arrived in the yard outside, a white Rolls-Royce, flying a pennant. Parviz was staring through the window at it.

'How many of you are holed up in this country?' McGovern was asking, again without reply from Parviz. McGovern looked at the photograph of old Vaziree on the wall. 'Who is he?'

'My father.'

'Where is he?'

'He is dead.'

'Dead where?'

'Back home.'

McGovern pointed to another of the faces on the group photograph. 'And him?'

'I believe he also is dead.'

'Where?'

'I have no idea.'

Morgan could see the face on the photograph – Sirus – and remembered the particulars from his Sunday afternoon in the archives. 'He was killed in Paris,' he said. Parviz and Laleh looked at him in surprise. 'Shot in broad daylight outside his apartment with his two bodyguards. The two bodyguards were killed. He died in an American military hospital ten days later. The French newspapers never carried the story.'

McGovern tapped the photograph again. 'There's seven of you here. Who's the girl?'

'Mr Vaziree has been locked up for three years,' said Laleh suddenly. 'How do you expect him to know where they all are?'

'It's my job to ask, Mrs Colraine.' McGovern slipped the photograph back in the pile of letters and papers on the bunk. Morgan could see Pike picking his way round the puddles to the caravan door. McGovern was leafing through the rest of the letters and papers.

'Man from the embassy is here,' said Pike through the open door, and as McGovern looked round at the door Morgan slipped the photograph into his own pocket.

'What embassy?' asked Parviz.

'Your friend's belongings will be sent back to his next of kin.'

'You can't do that.' Parviz picked up the papers on the table. 'We are his next of kin. I am his next of kin.' There was sudden urgency in his voice.

McGovern took the papers from his hand. 'He had a wife and children. You read the letter.'

'This is not for them,' said Parviz. 'There are names of people in here. People at home. People they could arrest and torture.' Parviz made a grab for the letters on the bunk. McGovern stepped forward to stand in his way, then turned to Pike. 'Get him out of here.'

Dorff pushed past Pike to grab Parviz by one arm and pull him down the caravan steps out into the drizzle.

'*I'm* not Amnesty International, Mrs Colraine,' said McGovern in apparent answer to an unspoken question. Morgan couldn't see her expression. They were both watching Parviz trip and stumble in the puddles as Dorff marched him past the white Rolls-Royce to the police van. The electric window in the rear of the Rolls slid up. It seemed to Morgan that Parviz had spat at the car as he passed.

McGovern was losing his limited patience. Twice he'd been through the letters and papers. He turned his

79

attention now to the books so carefully arranged above the window. He flicked through the pages of the first book, turned it upside down and shook it.

Morgan suddenly knew what McGovern was going to do – premonition or *déjà vu* or Laleh's account of the night her father had been killed. He almost reached out to take the book away. McGovern held the book in both hands and tore it in half down the spine.

A 'No!' in pained protest came from Laleh.

McGovern took down another book, flicked the pages, turned it upside down, then again with both hands ripped it apart.

'You don't have to do that!' Laleh's voice was raised. She turned to Morgan: 'He doesn't have to do that.'

McGovern took down a third book.

'Please,' she said to Morgan. 'Will you stop him doing that.'

'Mr Giugiardini and I used to work together, madam,' said McGovern. 'But I no longer take orders from him.'

As he tore the third book in half, Laleh turned away through the open door.

'Names and addresses,' said McGovern. 'Telephone numbers. He kept them somewhere.'

'In his head maybe.' Morgan was watching Laleh through the window as she picked her angry way round the puddles and across the yard. She was walking back to McGovern's white Rover but changed her mind and turned instead to the police van where Parviz was once more locked inside. Only this time Dorff had left the key in the door. She unlocked and opened it. Parviz reached out a hand to help her into the van.

Morgan looked back at McGovern, who was still intent on his destruction of Farshid's little library. Seven books, most of which McGovern would doubtless have called subversive, were now torn in half and scattered on the floor. He'd found nothing. He looked round at Morgan.

'Farshid Sabet was living here for eighteen months,'

said Morgan, 'and you didn't even know he was in the country. That's what really bugs you, isn't it?' Morgan stood up and walked the two paces to the door. 'Maybe you're not tapping enough pay-phones, McGovern.'

4

It was a dour and silent carload driving through the rain on the motorway back into town: McGovern, an uncomfortable sandwich between Morgan and Laleh on the back seat, and Laleh, uncommunicative, staring out of the window at the spray from lorries on the inner lanes.

Morgan had made the mistake of asking her what Parviz had been talking about in the van. 'Nothing that concerns any of you,' she'd replied. 'I will not be used as a spy.'

Not surprising, perhaps, that Morgan was not invited in out of the rain this evening, though to be fair to Laleh he hadn't made it clear whether or not or for how long he intended to lurk in her garden. And she, once indoors and with a fire lit, sat there in the gathering dusk without moving from her chair, even to draw the curtains. She couldn't have known he was still out there, and the one time she did move to go briefly upstairs, Morgan was sheltering out of sight behind the garage and only knew she had moved when he heard water from a bathroom.

There was the stillness of a late summer night drenched in drizzle and mist, and the smell of apples in the neighbouring garden. Morgan hunched himself into the donkey jacket, a check-list in his mind of unanswered questions from an hour on a card-phone in Euston Station that morning. He'd played journalist with a girl on the switchboard at the American Embassy and found out that Laleh's husband, Caleb Colraine, was a very senior person there. An extremely high-flying career diplomat with two sons at an English prep school, according to the girl, and a decorative wife who spoke five languages. Morgan had also called Paris and asked them to run a check on Farshid Sabet, not knowing that the exiled journalist was already dead. Paris's check had come up with very little. Interpol was not officially interested in politicians who did not have a criminal record. A lonely death the man had died. Morgan was quite sure it had also been violent and terrifying.

A car stopped on the road outside and he moved to keep the gate in view, his head just above the level of the top steps at the side of the house. No sign of anyone; Mr Caleb Colraine was late this evening.

Morgan pulled the green phone-cards out of his pocket and wondered, looking at them, if those pretty French accountants in St Cloud would pass them through expenses. Thirty quid he'd spent on Euston Station: four days' rent at Frau Luethi's in Lugano. I've even stopped wishing I was back there, he thought. I could be hibernating with the computer as autumn closes in round the mountains. He actually knew exactly when he had stopped thinking of Lugano and his abandoned list of bank accounts. It had been the moment in the prison that first morning when Parviz Vaziree had walked through the door in his dirty sandalled feet smelling like the parrot house in the zoo. A little spark of anger had ignited at the back of Morgan's heart or mind or soul, all of which he had long presumed fireproof.

He hadn't heard the car door slam out in the street.

The street was empty, the half-dozen parked cars were also empty.

The sixth sense that sane people call paranoia.

Morgan felt the wet on his shoes as he moved off the steps and path onto the lawn at the back of the house. He already guessed that the gate in the end wall had opened and closed. A pity he couldn't see the hand in the darkness that closed round the piece of ironstone at the side of the rockery.

Not a weapon. The ironstone was lobbed underarm into the shrubbery, a crash that drew Morgan to the far side of the lawn while his adversary ran lightly and silently down the near side of the lawn and up the iron stairs to the kitchen door. The door had opened, closed and was locked before Morgan could reach it. A moment later all the lights in the house went out.

Laleh had no idea how long she'd been sitting there; dusk had now turned to darkness. Sometime she must have fed the fire; once been upstairs and returned with the photograph in the silver frame from her dressing-table in the bedroom. The light was on in the hall.

When she heard the back door open and close her initial alarm was that Cal was home and dinner unprepared.

'Cal – is that you?' she called out. But there was no reply. Only the sound of someone moving in the kitchen. A moment later the hall light went out. Laleh could date her terror of darkness from the night her father had died twenty-seven years ago: she, a six-year-old girl, was walking down the stone passage to the one lit room and the voices upraised in anger; the sound of firing; and the lights fusing as her father fell and dragged the lamp with him to the floor. She'd been reliving that night in her head all evening. It was a miracle she stopped herself screaming now. For a moment she suddenly pictured last night's dead man illuminated as he must have been in the lonely telephone-kiosk on that country lane. I must move, she thought. Whoever is there can see where I'm sitting silhouetted against the glow of the fire.

She took the heavy poker and felt her way to the nearer of the two doors, her hand tapping the wall to find the light switch. None of the lights were working

84

and the hall and stairs outside were pitch dark. Her arm, upraised with the poker, was trembling, ready to swing at the first sound or touch of the intruder, her terror of darkness now compounded by the silence, like a wall around her. The outside world had vanished – the street lamps and passing cars and the slap of water in the canal across the road.

Then she did hear sounds from outside: someone hurrying, perhaps falling, on the steps at the side of the house. She had no further temptation to flee through the front door if there was someone else lurking outside. Her foot stubbed on the step up to the kitchen. As she half-stumbled through the doorway she felt a hand grab her head, covering her mouth, another hand pluck away the poker.

'Don't scream, lovely lady,' said a voice in her ear.

She did scream, through the hand on her mouth, trying to fight herself free of the man.

'Hey, it's me,' said the voice in her ear and the two arms turned her into Roundie's laughing face, a little shamed by her terror. 'I'm sorry, Lal,' he whispered. 'Bad joke. I just wanted to prove your bodyguard's no damn good.'

Someone was ringing the bell at the front door and banging the knocker. Lal subsided into a chair, still shaking, watching Roundie draw the curtains in the darkness. Again she heard the scrabbling of footsteps on the wet and slippery steps outside. Her bodyguard.

'It's the Irish in me,' Roundie apologized again and restored the lights at the mains as outside the someone banged on the back door. Laleh heard Morgan's voice.

'Mrs Colraine!'

'It's all right,' she called out.

'Laleh!'

'I'm all right,' she repeated. 'It's a friend – playing a joke.'

Roundie grinned, apologetic again, then raised his

eyebrows at the voice outside. 'Sounds like your bird-dog's fallen in love with you.'

Twice Morgan had slipped on those sodding steps. His trousers were wet and dirty, blood, he guessed, on one knee, and the drizzle was running down the inside of his collar as he turned away.

5

'I take it all men still *do* fall in love with you.' Roundie had closed the sitting-room curtains and turned to Laleh as she sat again in the chair by the fire. He looked down at her shoes propped by the fender, muddy from the farmyard that afternoon. 'Where have you been? Digging graves?' Roundie prodded at the fire with the poker he was still carrying, set the poker down and cocked his head at Laleh. 'You've been crying.'

Laleh was silent.

'Did I frighten you?'

Laleh nodded at the suggested explanation. 'Yes, Roundie, you frightened me.'

Roundie picked up the photograph of Laleh's father in its silver frame. 'You were sitting here in the dark. That's when you were crying.'

Roundie replaced the photograph on the table.

'Someone died last night.' Laleh looked up at him.

'A friend?' asked Roundie.

'A friend to whom I have never spoken.'

'Died how?'

'Dropped down dead, they say.'

Roundie walked over to the piano.

'Do you believe in coincidence?' asked Laleh.

Roundie laughed. 'A journalist believes only in coincidence. And in cock-ups.' Roundie turned to her from the piano. 'Hey!'

Laleh looked up and smiled at him. Practical jokes apart, he was a good soul to have around at bad times;

part of the cement that held her and Cal together, their drunken evenings together scattered over the last twelve years from New York to Santiago, Washington to Rome, Saigon to London.

The sound of the piano drowned the car outside and the key in the latch a moment later.

Roundie was still watching Laleh as he played. 'Decided you married the wrong man yet?' The expression on his face for once denied his smile. But then he grinned again. 'Cal couldn't play the piano to save his life.'

Cal walked in from the hall with a cool nod for them both and looked down at the hearth. 'You've mud on your shoes, Lal.'

Morgan walked out into the street leaving the sound of the piano behind. He'd already guessed one of the parked cars twenty yards up the street was a beige Metro. Morgan ran his pencil-beam torch over the inside of the car: a folder of Avis documents on the floor; a couple of maps; an empty cigarette packet and an ashtray full of dog-ends. Sweet Aftons, this Mr Curtiss smoked, if Ralph Curtiss he really was. 'An old friend,' Laleh had said. 'A journalist.' Morgan hadn't yet told her he'd seen Mr Curtiss outside Winson Green the morning Farshid had been there. The day Farshid had been killed.

Morgan tried four phone-boxes and was halfway across Maida Vale before he found one that worked. He rang Directory Enquiries for the Avis number, wiping rain off his face and neck with a handkerchief as he dialled the number and talked to the girl on the car-hire desk. 'Met traffic here, love. Can you run a check on one of your cars. It's blocking a hotel gateway and I don't want to have to tow it away. If you give me the hirer's name I can have him paged.'

'Who did you say you were?' asked the girl.

'Metropolitan Police, Traffic Division. A beige Metro.' Morgan gave her the car registration number and waited while she tapped it up on a computer or looked it up in files.

A car turned into the street behind him, headlamps approaching slowly, dazzling him as he looked round. Like Laleh earlier, Morgan had a sudden vision of Farshid illuminated in that lonely kiosk down the country lane. He remembered the tyre-marks on the verge.

The car had stopped five yards away down the street, headlights pointing at him. It was seven years since anyone had taken a shot at him but Morgan swore he heard the sound of a gun - and ducked. I haven't come home to die in a dirty London phone-box, he thought. Then laughed at his moment of fear as the car turned away and the Avis girl came back on the line.

'Panmeridian Press,' she said. 'We don't have the name of the actual client driving it.'

That feeling of fear or unease lingered as he zigzagged back into town through the empty and quiet backwaters of St John's Wood and Marylebone where pursuit or a tail were easier to detect.

'Jumpy ain't you, ducky?' Beth laughed at him, waving a hand of cards in her fingerless mittens at the mirror on the wall behind her. Morgan heard the pub door bang open again, his ears tuned to it over the sound of the jazz. Again he glanced up at the mirror to check the faces coming in. And again Beth cackled at him. 'Who are you frightened of this time, ducky? Cops or robbers?'

'Shadows, Beth. I'm getting long in the tooth.'

6

The phone rang an hour after supper. Ashley was out of his chair like the sprinter he once had been, to beat Jasper to the door. Not that Jasper even bothered to move. Brother and niece had been in the house a week now and every single phone call had been made or received by them.

Annie upstairs had also jumped up, red rose in her hand from the bedside table in the box room, red petals on the bed where she'd been shredding it. She opened the door and tiptoed to the head of the stairs.

'Hello, Hugh,' she heard her father say. 'We had a word this morning. I think he may be ready to talk.'

That's all it was: 'Hello, Hugh'; a few words; and down went the phone. Transatlantic, Annie guessed. It was three o'clock in Washington. Ashley looked up and saw her watching him over the bannisters.

Her words were spat at him: 'You bugger!'

7

'Two hours you were watching that pub mirror this evening.' Rudi drained spaghetti over the sink and served out two plates. 'Like Papa used to watch the shop door on Friday afternoons waiting for the heavies to walk in and help themselves to their protection money out of the till.' Rudi carried the plates to the table, Morgan making room for him.

'Every Friday afternoon dressing the shop window so he could watch the street. And dodging in and out of the bloody loo every ten minutes like you in the pub this evening.'

'That's old age, little brother.' Morgan rolled a fork of spaghetti, sniffed and tasted it. '*Prezzemolo, aglio, olio, vino,*' he said lightly. '*E vongole.*'

Rudi was not in the mood to discuss his clam sauce, sitting down at the table without a smile. Morgan poured him a glass of wine, watching him for a moment. 'It wasn't that Papa was frightened of them, you know. What hurt him was if *we* saw them helping themselves out of his till – or if one of his customers saw them. He wasn't frightened. He was shamed.'

Rudi was watching him like the little brother Morgan remembered all those years ago. 'And that's why you've been looking for them ever since, in a manner of speaking.'

Morgan laughed. 'You were the one who went for them, Rudi. Eleven years old, with the Parmesan chisel, the week Papa was in hospital?'

'Then one of them hit me and you picked up the knife and they walked out.'

'And came back a week later for compensation.' Morgan shook his head. 'You eventually find out it's not the gorillas on the street you're after. It's the someone else who's behind them all. Or the someone elses behind the someone else.'

'Do you ever find them?'

Morgan shook his head again.

'If you did, what would you do? Kill them?'

Morgan picked up Rudi's fork and slipped it into his brother's hand. 'Come on, kid. You're meant to be eating your dinner.'

'*Would* you kill them?'

Morgan laughed. 'I'm a statistician, Rudi. I don't kill people. I don't even carry a gun.'

My kid brother, thought Morgan. Giving up his bed and sleeping on the floor and waiting, every time I come to stay, for trouble to follow me up the stairs. Morgan looked over his shoulder through the door at Rudi asleep on his bed of newspapers. He sucked at his pipe, turning pages in the red box-file looking for the thread he'd missed, or the faces or names, the someone elses behind the someone else.

He'd had copies made of the photograph 'borrowed' from the caravan that afternoon and laid one out now on Rudi's kitchen table with the newspaper cutting that had identified so precisely its place and time in history. A press photographer had taken that group picture at an airport down on the Gulf, minutes, maybe even seconds before old Vaziree had been assassinated six years ago. Morgan drew a cross in red ink over the old man's face; then over his neighbour – Sirus, who'd been killed in Paris. A red ink circle round Parviz, standing in the photograph with a girl – a rather beautiful girl. Who? Another red ink cross for Farshid.

Morgan heard a sound on the stairs outside – 'oral French' or 'schoolgirl' seeing off a client? Morgan turned, looking through the other room at the door. The handle was turning slowly, quietly, eventually blocked by the lock.

Morgan pushed the red file and photographs into his bag, waved a hand ineffectually at the pipe smoke and pulled open the skylight above Rudi's bed of newspapers in the next room. He threw his bag out onto the roof and pulled himself up to follow as the someone outside thumped on the door. Unseen by Morgan, the photograph he'd been doodling on with the red pen fell to the floor.

Rudi woke at the second round of thumping. He jumped, startled and naked, to his feet, looking up at the open skylight and pulling it shut. His voice trembled as he asked through the door: 'Who is it?'

Morgan could see his brother, through the skylight, pulling a cover from the bed to wrap round himself before easing open the door.

'Where's your brother?' Morgan heard the Smethwick whine and saw his brother's fear as he backed away.

'He's not here.' Rudi's voice was still trembling.

McGovern walked through to the kitchen. 'Smoke a pipe in your sleep, do you?'

They were out of Morgan's line of sight, but the voices were still faintly audible through the roof.

Down below Rudi had seen the photograph and guessed its possible significance. With McGovern's back still turned in the kitchen he kicked it to one side under the chest of drawers.

'Sleeping on the floor, Rudi?' McGovern returned to the other room.

'Wet the bed, didn't I,' Rudi replied.

McGovern pulled open one of the drawers in the chest of drawers. Rudi blocked it with his hand and shut it again. 'Do you have a warrant?' he asked.

McGovern looked almost startled. 'Well, well.

Someone's been giving Rudolph a lesson in his citizen's rights.' McGovern pulled the drawer open again and up-ended it over the floor. 'Don't play games with me, Rudi. I can have you done for dealing any time I want.'

'I'm not a pusher. You know that.'

'When it comes to justice, Rudolph, it's not a question of what actually occurred, but what you can get the court to believe. The planting of evidence is one of the few weapons left to the police in our unremitting war on crime.' McGovern picked a joss-stick out of a jar and sniffed at it, then looked up at the skylight and pulled it open. 'Tell your brother,' he shouted up, 'I want the photograph he took from the caravan this afternoon.' His voice dropped a tone. 'I'd hate to have to turn this place over.' McGovern pulled a bra out of the mess of clothes from the drawer now scattered on the floor. 'I don't really enjoy your sad little secrets.' McGovern turned at the door, his voice raised again at the open skylight: 'Your brother spent too many years infiltrating terrorists. He's picked up their nasty habits. It's time he was put out to grass.'

Morgan watched the street below from the roof – Pike was by the white Rover, McGovern climbing in and slamming his door shut.

Rudi, picking the drawerful of clothes off the floor, was still shaking when Morgan dropped himself back through the open skylight.

Morgan tried a laugh. 'Doesn't have much finesse, does he?'

Rudi did not reply.

Morgan rescued his brother's old instrument case out of the rubble on the floor – the shining flute and piccolo that were Rudi's original pride and joy. The clarinet in the jazz band had started as a Sunday joke.

'He bust you from the orchestra again, didn't he?'

Rudi looked up at his brother. 'Pulled me on a drugs charge.'

'Last time I was here?'

94

'Not long after. Twice in my life I snort coke and the second time he has to find me with it. Once you're coloured with hard stuff none of the orchestras will touch you.' Rudi slid the photograph from under the chest of drawers and handed it up. 'Is that what he was looking for?'

Morgan stared at it.

'What's with the noughts and crosses?'

Rudi boiled a kettle to make some tea.

'Crosses for the dead,' said Morgan. 'Noughts for those still alive. Six men and a girl – the girl seems to belong to Parviz Vaziree. When the photograph was taken they were returning to Teheran from a political rally. Moments after it was taken the old man was killed. Then the priests took over and within a few months the party was scattered, some in exile, some in prison. Sirus' – Morgan pointed to another of the red crosses – 'was shot in Paris. The others all disappeared until the where-abouts of only one was known.' He indicated the circle round Parviz. 'A prison camp. Last Sunday he was let out at the end of a long string and lo and behold one of the other three appeared and, it seems, dropped dead from sheer surprise.' The cross was over Farshid. Morgan circled the other two – Sasan and Shaheenee. 'No one knows where *they* are, nor whether they'll have the good sense to stay in hiding.'

8

At Heathrow that early morning, Parviz bowed his head to the sunrise through the window and prayed that no one else would step from the shadows out of hiding.

In Milan as that same sunrise melted mist in the cathedral square a young Iranian girl, Firuze, did step from shadow into sunlight to cross the piazza. She was small and slight, simply dressed and unadorned, and very beautiful. She bought a dozen newspapers under the colonnade, Italian, French, German, English and Arabic – then walked to the old Campari bar on the corner of the *galleria* where the waiter was putting out tables in the sunshine. She stood at the bar and ordered two coffees.

A hundred yards away in the SIP office at the far end of the *galleria,* one of the two circled faces on the noughts and crosses photograph was sitting in front of a line of telephone cubicles waiting for a call that never came. The clerk behind one of the desks crossing off his requested number as Sasan looked at his watch, shrugged at her and walked out into the vaulted arcade. The telephone clerks were used to the regular faces – Ethiopians, Iranians, Palestinians, Poles – exiles and refugees gathering by the telephones from early morning with the old men who used the office more as a club, a place of warmth to sit and talk and hope that someone would eventually leave unclaimed money in one of the pay-phones that lined the wall. The old men took it in turn to check the phones as each client left, discreetly nudging the yellow button and listening for the money to fall.

Sasan walked down the coloured marble pavement. Two full-dress *carabinieri* were at the end of the *galleria*, swords and cocked hats silhouetted against the sunlight in the piazza.

Sasan was frightened, both by what he intended to do and what he had heard on the BBC World Service news in the middle of last night.

Firuze had already seen it in that morning's Italian newspapers – a small agency report, nothing more. Announcing the death of an exiled journalist in England. Farshid.

'I have a flight in one hour's time,' Sasan told her.

'That's exactly what they want you to do,' she said. 'Why else would they have reported this?' Her voice was low and urgent. 'They're using the newspapers to draw you out.'

'Someone has to warn Parviz,' said Sasan. 'If he makes the wrong move now, it will be finished for all of us.'

'Please don't go,' she whispered.

'Look after Shaheenee,' he said. '*Khoda negahdar.*' *God protect you.*

9

When they stayed in Oxford, Ashley was always the first to move in the morning, as soon as he heard the newspaper boy on his bike. He knew how Jasper hated to find the *Guardian* contaminating his *Telegraph* on the doormat.

Farshid's photograph on the back page pulled Ashley up short, an involuntary mutter of anger as he immediately assumed the worst. 'DEATH OF EXILED JOURNALIST'. The 'natural causes' did not convince him, and he knew would not convince Annie.

He carried the paper up to her bedroom, remembering with some foreboding her outburst of yesterday evening. Her room was empty and the bed unslept in. For a moment Ashley thought she might have left during the night. He glanced through the window, but the car was still there, axle-deep in the long grass on the front lawn. He crossed the landing to try the box-room door, and sure enough she was in there on the bed made up the previous night for Parviz – hugged to the pillow and fast asleep.

He covered her bare shoulder with the blanket; touched a strand of her hair on the pillow; but did not wake her, leaving the paper folded to the back-page picture of Farshid on the bedside table under the one surviving and fading red rose.

How much, he thought, his daughter reminded him of her mother: red hair and Celtic anger; soft white skin and that wonderful capacity for laughter and tears.

★

'I need to request a second autopsy in the UK,' said Morgan into the phone, trying not to shout over the music. He looked at his watch. 'On a body due for cremation in four hours' time.'

The girl started muttering in French at him over the crackle on the line. Perhaps Interpol's threatened move to a new office in Lyons would improve the quality, if not of the ancillary girls, certainly of the telephones.

'Legal department,' he told the girl. 'I need to know what the hell I do about it.' Morgan looked through the Perspex bubble of the pay-phone at Rudi, sitting cross-legged in the middle of St Martin's Court gazing rapt at the two buskers, flute and violin, playing Bach.

Morgan made the girl repeat what he had said and told her he would call back from another phone in twenty minutes' time. If I can find another British Telecom public phone that actually works, he thought to himself.

He pulled Rudi to his feet and tossed a coin into the violin case.

'You know, they also tap pay-phones,' said Rudi.

Morgan grinned: 'Only on a random basis.'

For the second consecutive day in Birmingham the *magistrato* had been deprived of his witness and had to make do with Veltri and the solicitor on their own. Assuntino was beginning to feel the likelihood of extradition slip away; and even beginning to wonder who the hell had put this case together in the first place.

And, like Morgan, he had begun to ask himself whether there weren't other motives behind the temporary release of this Parviz Vaziree.

10

The crematorium looked cheerful under the sunshine with its laid-out rose gardens and flowering shrubs for all seasons.

Morgan had chosen a seat on one of the lawns from where he could see both chapel and car park. Catalogue the mourners, he thought.

Laleh was the first to arrive. The taxi dropped her by the chapel and moved into the car park to wait. She was carrying flowers. Morgan had not been expecting her.

He watched her examine a line of wreaths and called across the silent garden to her. 'They were for the two o'clock bonfire. We're here for the three o'clock.'

She looked round in surprise.

'Is this part of the job,' he went on. 'Or are you representing the embassy?'

She seemed bewildered both by his question and his tone of voice.

'I came,' she replied, 'out of respect.'

Morgan walked over to her. 'You will claim expenses for this afternoon, I imagine.'

Laleh looked at him in astonishment. 'Meaning?'

'Meaning, I've been wondering who is paying you.'

'The Italians.'

'How come they asked for you?' He could sense her begin to bristle.

'My three languages are not always easy to find together.'

'I checked with an agency,' said Morgan. 'They had seven names on their books for your three languages. And anyway, Parviz Vaziree speaks perfect English.'

She stared at him for a moment in silence. 'Are you interrogating me?'

'I'm asking questions. I'm curious.'

Another moment of silence while she looked at him. 'I don't have to answer questions from you.'

'No.'

She was still looking at him, hurt or offended. 'I'm a professional,' she said. 'I do my job. It's a technical job. I'm not doing it *for* anyone.' Her anger was flowing now. 'You think I'm here today because I'm working for someone? I'm here because Farshid Sabet came from my mother's country, and because he was alone when he died, and because what has happened is sad.' There were tears in her eyes as she turned away and Morgan wished he hadn't had to use quite so much needle to draw her out. At least, he thought, her sympathies are identified; and, he hoped, her innocence.

Both their faces had been framed and focused in a long telephoto lens – an SLR wrapped in a sweater to muffle the sound of its motorized shutter. That same machine now began to record a quick succession of arrivals as three o'clock approached: a blue police van with Parviz and his minders; the white police Rover with Pike and McGovern, McGovern's Smethwick whine clearly audible across the flower-beds – 'funny bloody place for a Muslem burial'; then, in something of a rush, a battered yellow Renault that hurtled down the entrance drive to park, and both Morgan and the telephoto lens watched Ashley and Annie walking quickly to the chapel. Morgan recognized the girl from the noughts and crosses picture.

Another taxi had arrived on the road, out of sight and

unrecorded, pulling onto the grass verge to wait as the hearse itself turned into the gate. Morgan, waiting like the priest for the coffin to arrive, did not notice the new arrival. Only the telephoto lens, focusing from shrub to rose garden to cover both back and front of the chapel, picked up the figure of Sasan as he moved swiftly from the taxi and crossed the further lawns towards the rear of the chapel, while the hearse drew in under the portico.

The hearse was empty but for wreaths; no coffin, no body. The young priest was confused and agitated as he read the note passed to him by the driver. Morgan followed him into the chapel, the funeral musak cutting out as the priest pushed a button and prepared to address the scattering of mourners.

In that moment the door opened to admit the last of them. Each head turned to look as Sasan slipped inside.

'I'm very sorry to have to tell you,' said the shy young priest, 'this service cannot proceed.' He referred to the note. 'The body of Mr Farshid Sabet has been withheld for a further post-mortem.'

Morgan was conscious of McGovern's head turning to glare at him.

'Regrettably, this decision was made too late to inform anyone.'

The clergyman folded away his note and looked at them. 'I can only offer my sincere sympathy for what must be not only inconvenient but distressing for you all.' He turned away. McGovern and Pike followed him into the office.

Parviz broke away from his pew, eluding Dorff, talking loudly in Farsi or Arabic as he walked quickly to Sasan at the back of the chapel. The two of them embraced. Both of them talked with a desperate urgency, but Dorff was already at Parviz's shoulder, trying to pull him away.

Whatever Sasan was saying seemed to anger Parviz.

He was shouting at his old friend and colleague as Dorff and the CID man walked him to the door.

Morgan crossed the aisle to where Laleh was sitting. 'What were they saying?' he asked her. Predictably she turned away without a reply.

'*Khosh Amadid*. It is good to see you.' A careful English voice greeted Sasan at the back of the chapel: the elderly man with the red-headed girl from the battered yellow Renault. 'We had no way of communicating with any of you.'

'How did he die?' asked Sasan.

'It would seem he had a stroke. Though that is now apparently subject to a second opinion.'

Sasan turned to the girl and kissed her hand. 'The few times we meet,' he said, 'the circumstances are always unfortunate.' Sasan was watching the door. 'Shaheenee would have said to greet you. I'm sorry, I cannot say more. We have been reduced to secrecy and concealment.'

Sasan took Ashley by the hand. 'If you can, do something for Parviz. He should not be allowed to go back.'

'We need to be able to make contact with you and Shaheenee,' said Ashley.

'That is and must remain impossible,' replied Sasan, and turned away down the aisle through a rear door back into the sunlight outside. Small, neat and precise – the only member of their party who had, however, briefly, gained the ear of the Shah in the years before revolution.

Morgan followed Sasan out into the sunlight and watched him cut across the lawns and shrubs away from the car park and drive. Morgan guessed he'd left a car or taxi out on the road.

The white Rover pulled up alongside Morgan halfway to the gate, and McGovern's window was wound down. 'Next time you want a private autopsy, you ask me first.'

'*You* should have asked for it twenty-four hours ago,' replied Morgan, and pulled the borrowed photograph from his bag. 'Yours, I believe.'

McGovern did not offer him a lift. No more did Laleh as she passed him in her taxi.

Morgan turned up the road outside the gate, resigned to a long walk.

11

It was later established that Sasan paid off his taxi at Twyford Station some time between 3.45 and four o'clock that afternoon. He showed the return half of a ticket from Reading at the barrier, and for whatever reason chose to wait not on the centre platform where his train would arrive, but on the far platform, sitting on a bench from which he could see the station entrance across the intervening tracks and platform. It was also later confirmed that a high-sided trolley full of mail-bags was parked to one side of the bench where he was sitting.

'THIS IS A STATION ANNOUNCEMENT. PLEASE STAND CLEAR OF THE PLATFORM EDGE. A FAST TRAIN IS APPROACHING.'

Twice the announcement was made in as many minutes, once for the up-line Plymouth to Paddington train running on time, once for the down-line Paddington to Bristol train running seven minutes late. Both these trains were travelling at one hundred and twenty-five m.p.h. a few yards in front of Sasan, each train taking barely three and a half seconds to pass him. Presumably some time during those six or seven seconds the two men, if not already on the station, entered the station unseen by him.

A few minutes later a second taxi arrived in the fore-court outside. Laleh Colraine had abandoned her return ticket from Bracknell to Waterloo, and settled for the Twyford train into Paddington, where she'd be only two or three minutes from home in a taxi. She had a dinner party to organize that evening for fifty people.

Both Laleh, in the booking office, and Sasan on the far platform may then have been conscious of the branch-line train from Henley pulling into the bay platform, the loud-speaker apologizing for its late arrival. 'Cows on the line.'

An old lady off the Henley train was much encumbered by bags and parcels, one of which she dropped. Glancing across the station she saw, or later thought she'd seen, two men approach Sasan, pushing another of the high-sided mail-bag trolleys.

It was at this moment that a third station announcement warned of the approach of another fast train – the down-line Paddington to Penzance running to time.

Only Farshid would have recognized the slim-built Arab with the moustache and the burning dark eyes, and Farshid was dead. Sasan, looking up at the trolley moving towards him and the face that appeared from behind it, only recognized danger and perhaps for a moment even anticipated death.

A second man grabbed him from behind, the first immobilizing Sasan as he had immobilized Farshid, with one very precise blow to the solar plexus. Winded and momentarily paralysed, Sasan could only watch as the man pulled the air ticket from his inner pocket.

The old lady had heard, or thought she'd heard, a shout. She was looking again across the station at the three men on the far platform. The train was now only a few seconds away under the bridge on the London side of the station, airhorn blasting as it exploded into and through the station.

The driver had a split-second glimpse of two or perhaps three men struggling as they appeared from behind a mail-bag trolley. Then one of the men tipped headlong off the platform under the nose of the train. The driver, shouting in his cab, hit the emergency brakes. He stopped forty seconds later one mile down the track, his screen obscured by substance that looked like a light-coloured mud.

In the booking office, Laleh, unaware of what had happened, had bought her ticket and walked to the gate. The killer and his colleague passed her at the gate, aware of each other – a spark of recognition between the Arab men and the Persian lady.

PART THREE

'Caviar'

1

Morgan arrived at the hospital some forty minutes after McGovern. Sergeant Pike was a little shamefaced as he watched him push through the swing-doors into the corridor outside Pathology. 'Would have given you a lift if we'd known you were coming here,' he said lamely.

'I hope you like your game well hung,' was all Mc-Govern said as Morgan walked past them both to the door of the theatre. Clearly, the two policemen had no stomach for what was going on inside.

The pathologist glanced up from his saws and scalpels as Morgan entered. He was working on the heart, holding it clear of the body as he sliced a cross-section out of it. 'I take it you're the Interpol man,' he said.

Morgan nodded.

The patho pointed a scalpel at the desk in the corner. 'You have some papers and statements to sign for the local coroner. He wasn't best pleased at having a PM challenged.'

The body on the slab was anonymous, Farshid's head covered. The pathologist worked on in silence for a few moments before speaking again, voice half-muffled in his face mask. 'Mind you, every time I see "vagal inhibition" on a death certificate I always assume it's been an escape diagnosis.' Another pause while he sliced out a section of coronary artery. 'Nothing much wrong with his heart,' he muttered. He looked round at Morgan. 'Bound to happen once or twice a year. No reflection on my colleague. You get someone's body that just won't tell you why it gave up its ghost. As far as you can see, the heart just stopped beating. Could take you six weeks to do all the tests so if no one's breathing down your neck – no insurance companies and no policemen – you might just use "vagal inhibition" and leave it at that.'

'Sounds vaguely obscene,' said Morgan.

The pathologist laughed. 'Pneumogastric nerve. It services the heart. Keeps it thudding away.' The pathologist looked up at McGovern's face frowning through the window in the door and wondering what they could be laughing about.

'I imagine Special Branch thinks I'm trying to influence your decision,' said Morgan.

'And are you?'

'Good heavens no.'

The pathologist was taking specimen shavings of tissue for his slides. 'But no doubt you have a theory, otherwise you and I would not be here with this already much abused corpse.'

'More a memory than a theory,' said Morgan. 'We have it on file somewhere. An Arab terrorist about nine years ago in Munich who apparently died from natural causes but was subsequently thought to have been knocked off by the Israelis. He was eventually exhumed – a little wormeaten, but they found a hypodermic puncture under the hair at the back of the neck. They did chemical analysis. Unfortunately, it was too long since death to establish anything. There were two theories – either some sort of liquid gas rather like an aerosol to compress the brain and then disperse –'

The pathologist looked over his mask. 'A little far-fetched, I think.'

'The second theory, a massive dose of concentrated insulin.'

The pathologist put aside what he was doing and looked at Morgan. 'Nasty,' he said. 'We'll have to put that one into the textbooks. It's a rather good way of getting rid of your mother-in-law.' He called for a cup of tea down the telephone, sewed up Farshid's front with mail-bag stitches, and uncovered his head to shave what was left of his beard and the back of his neck. 'Bleeding's the trouble in the head,' he said. 'You have to find somewhere you can paint on coagulant where no one's going to find it.'

But there was no sign of puncture or laceration on the back of Farshid's head. Morgan remembered the bearded giant outside the prison, now naked and shaven and sewn up like a boned and rolled joint of beef. He remembered also that Farshid had a wife, and two children who drew pictures of flowers.

'Ears, eyes, nose and mouth,' said the pathologist as the nurse pushed the door open with two cups of tea. Morgan had a glimpse of McGovern outside scowling through the door at him.

The pathologist took a scalpel and slit the soft flap of both nostrils up the line of the cheek. He inserted a tiny metal hook like a dentist's instrument, pushing it up to probe into the nasal cavity. The hook came out with a small plug of blooded cotton wool and wax.

'No idea yet what they used,' said the pathologist, explaining it to McGovern in the hospital car park. 'We'll do the chem tests – but even then there's no guarantee.'

'Suicide?' suggested McGovern.

The pathologist looked at him without reply and turned to Morgan. 'Fascinating,' he said. 'Bloody great puncture halfway through the cribriform. Veterinary needle, I'd say. With a lot of coagulant in the cotton and the wax.' He shook hands. 'Fascinating,' he added again as he walked off to his car.

Sergeant Pike was so impressed he actually offered Morgan a lift back to town without as much as a by-your-leave to McGovern.

2

One hour and a half they'd kept Laleh on the station until she finally convinced them she had been in the booking office when the accident or incident had happened.

'Everything under control?' called out Cal as he opened the front door with the first of the ambassador's handmaidens.

'Nothing's under control,' replied Laleh. 'The bloody trains were late. Some idiot threw himself under one.'

The old lady was pale and very tired. She'd been answering questions now for three and a half hours – first the stationmaster, then the local police, now the railway police. Each time she had repeated her account without change of detail or emphasis. Not that she wasn't used after so many years to being treated not only as old but as a woman. She was trying very hard not to lose her temper.

'Where's the driver?' the senior railway policeman asked the stationmaster.

'Taken to hospital suffering from shock.'

'A suicide is always hard on the driver.'

'It wasn't suicide,' said the old lady quietly.

The policeman looked up at her as another 125 hurtled past outside, the third in five minutes. 'Still trying to catch up the backlog,' the policeman said, looking at his watch. 'One-and-a-half-hours' track-time they lost here this afternoon.' He glared at the old lady as though it were somehow her fault. Stacked up all the way back to Wales and Cornwall. Timetable won't be right till tomorrow.' He glanced back at the notes he'd been reading. 'Did he pull his wire?' The airhorns, he meant.

The stationmaster nodded.

'What about the speed?'

'There's no speed checks this side of Slough,' said the constable. 'He was at maximum.'

'Wouldn't have seen the bloke till he actually threw himself, then.'

'He didn't throw himself,' said the old lady wearily. 'He was pushed.'

The senior policeman looked at her again. Reluctantly. 'So you say.' He looked down at the notes again. 'He was struggling, it says you said.'

'He had one man on each arm. They threw him.'

The policeman stood up suddenly. His Cardiff voice turned into Cardiff scrum-half. 'Grab me by the arms,' he told the other two – the reluctant constable and the tired stationmaster. 'I'm going forward,' he exhorted. 'You're trying to hold me back.'

The three of them swayed dangerously to and fro in the stationmaster's small office.

'Come on – fight me!' shouted the policeman, then suddenly banged his thigh against the desk and subsided. 'You see,' he said to the old lady. 'You can fight both ways, backwards and forwards. It looks much the same, wouldn't you say? Especially across four lines of railway tracks.'

'I don't wear glasses,' said the old lady. 'Only for reading.'

'Seems to me the two men might well have been trying to restrain him.'

'Is that what *they* are saying,' asked the old lady.

'They haven't found them yet, Mrs Baines,' said the stationmaster.

★

The police had taken a copy of the dead man's passport photograph for the local papers. 'Sandro Parise's the name,' the journalist was told. 'An Italian. Arrived in the country this morning, judging by the stamp in his passport. If you print the picture, someone round here might recognize him.'

'Bloody long way to come just to throw yourself under a train,' said the journalist.

3

It seemed to Annie she'd been on the road all day, pulling and pushing the gear-lever on her old Renault, her father carefully reticent in the seat beside her.

Common ground between them was dwindling – nothing much more than a shared concern for the safety and well-being of Parviz and Sasan. And Shaheenee, wherever he was hiding. Both father and daughter had heard those few hurried words between Parviz and Sasan at the crematorium and understood most of them, babbled though they had been in a deliberate confusion of Farsi and Arabic. Angry words that had indirectly spelt out to Annie and Ashley the two sides on which they both suspected the other was engaged. And yet that common ground, shrinking though it was, proved for the moment enough for mutual support. Especially for Annie, still moving in the dark.

After last night's skirmish with her father over the phone call, she had made her own first contact, as though to establish a deliberate counterbalance. Her father had spoken to Washington; then she, through old channels, would speak with Moscow. She knew her father would have guessed her move; what she didn't realize was how Ashley had gently manoeuvred her into making it, still with a hope in his mind that both sides would come to common agreement over the future of Parviz and his surviving colleagues.

They turned off the Westway at eight o'clock that evening, leaving a glowing sunset sky behind them as

Ashley tried to guide them through the maze of north Paddington streets he remembered from thirty years ago. Little Venice had never been so hard to find.

'Oh, Daddy!' Annie was exasperated as they made another wrong turn. And increasingly volatile as, however approximately, they approached their destination. Ashley had felt her slowly winding up all down the motorway. He was waiting for the first explosion. A minor one: 'I'd really rather spend the evening in a cinema,' she said. 'I'll come and pick you up when it's all over.'

'It's an excellent opportunity for you to meet the acceptable face of American diplomacy,' replied Ashley.

'Are they our lords and masters tonight?' she asked.

Ashley smiled: 'It's as well to let them think so.'

They found the right end of Blomfield Road and parked by the canal. The street was already well stacked with embassy limousines, Annie muttering to herself as she counted the Cadillacs and Rolls-Royces.

'What's that?' asked Ashley as they crossed the road.

'I said, Daddy, I do not guarantee to behave myself this evening.'

Laleh was surveying her tables of food when she saw them walk in and recognized them immediately from the crematorium that afternoon.

Cal had opened the door to them, leading them both to meet Hugh in the corner of the sitting-room – Blind Hugh, who'd arrived straight off Concorde an hour before, to brief Cal and Laleh about those unexpected and last-minute guests, 'natives' he'd called them.

Laleh listened now to the 'native' as he raised his voice to greet Hugh: 'Ashley Buchanan, Hugh. My daughter, Annie.'

'I'm blind, Ashley, not deaf.' Hugh frowned from his chair. Laleh saw Ashley smile and wink at his daughter. Cal beckoned Laleh across the crowded room.

118

'My wife, Laleh,' he said, introducing them. 'Ashley Buchanan and Annabel Buchanan.'

'I believe we all saw each other this afternoon,' smiled Laleh. Both Buchanans were clearly more surprised than she at the coincidence. 'My mother was Persian,' she explained, and turned her brilliant smile on Ashley. 'It is said you know more about my mother's country than most of the inhabitants themselves.'

'Ten or twenty years ago,' laughed Ashley. 'My expertise, if that is what it was, has been pensioned off.'

Laleh turned her smile to Annie. 'And I believe *you* wrote a book about the political situation before the – the change.'

'You're very well briefed,' said Annie defensively. 'Actually, it was more a pamphlet than a book.' She glanced at her father. 'And much frowned upon.'

Cal was still trying to work out the logistics. 'You were all at this funeral this afternoon?'

Roundie edged himself and a tray of glasses between Ashley and Annie. 'Screwdrivers or Bloody Marys,' he asked with a smile.

'There was no funeral,' said Laleh, to Cal's surprise. 'The body didn't turn up.'

Annie was watching Blind Hugh listening to them from his chair. 'Perhaps someone doesn't believe it died of natural causes,' she said.

Ashley corrected her: 'Now – we don't actually know that, Annie.'

Blind Hugh interposed: 'I thought it had been established that Farshid Sabet died from cardiac arrest. That's what it says in tomorrow's papers.'

'Tomorrow's newspapers must get to you very early,' said Annie.

A momentary pause before Hugh smiled, his face turning to the direction of her voice. 'I get the Braille edition, my dear. It's read to me over the telephone.'

Roundie laughed out loud, still hovering with his tray of cocktails. Cal led him away, hand under one elbow.

119

'Think we need some more glasses, Roundie. You were invited tonight to butler not to eavesdrop.'

'I'm a newsman,' laughed Roundie. 'I bin looking through keyholes all my life.' He nodded over his shoulder. 'I like your British Buchanans. Who invited them?'

'They sort of invited themselves – Mr Buchanan did, that is. With the help of Blind Hugh.'

Roundie shook his head as he walked through to the kitchen. 'You State Department guys – you really are a bunch of conspirators.'

Cal caught Laleh's eye across the crowded room, indicating with a nod that she should leave Hugh alone with the Buchanans. He followed Roundie into the kitchen, where the ambassador's borrowed handmaidens were heaping caviar round a mound of crushed ice.

Roundie wagged a finger as he watched. 'I shan't ask who smuggled that for you, Cal.'

Laleh walked in behind them. 'Who told Hugh about Farshid?' she asked, looking at her husband. He was peeling foil off a champagne bottle, untwisting the wire.

'You told me; I told him. Did I do wrong?'

Laleh watched him in silence, waiting for Roundie to pick up his new tray of glasses. Roundie winked at Laleh. 'Conspirators, all of you,' he whispered, as he left the room.

Laleh was still watching Cal. 'Where did you meet Ashley Buchanan?'

'I didn't meet him anywhere. I met him tonight. Blind Hugh thought he'd appreciate an invitation.' Cal was strangely defensive. 'As you said, dear, he's extremely knowledgeable about your mother's one-time homeland.' The champagne cork banged out, and Cal followed Roundie through to the sitting room.

Laleh watched him go and shook her head at herself. Morgan's paranoia was obviously contagious. She finished the garnish on the bowl of caviar and carried it into the sitting room to the predictable chorus of oohs and aahs. By the time she reached the table at the far end to set it down, the bowl was already surrounded, spoons clashing to scoop at the delicacy.

Annie watched them with disgust across the room as she listened to her father chatting up the blind man from Washington.

'Very significant that Sasan turned up today,' he was saying. 'He was always the closest to Shaheenee. It gives me hope that their party can regroup round Shaheenee and Parviz – the name of Vaziree is still very emotive. Maybe now they can emerge from the shadows.'

'Emerge from hiding, you mean, Father.' Annie was watching the mountain of caviar disappear.

'Whatever and wherever they're emerging from,' Blind Hugh was saying, 'it would be fruitful to talk with Shaheenee and with them all.'

'Before Parviz Vaziree is returned home,' said Ashley.

'Returned to prison, Father.'

4

Parviz couldn't actually see the planes landing or taking off through his barred window – he just glimpsed them between buildings, accelerating or decelerating along twenty yards or so of runway. Though he could, when it was dark and clear and when they were landing from the east, see the lights of incoming planes one behind the other, sometimes as many as four at a time stacked back towards London.

He could pray without distraction under their fearful roar; but not under the more gentle animal sounds of his German escort eating. Parviz was praying this evening, prostrate on the floor, when Dorff came back with their plastic boxes of chicken and chips. Embarrassed for a few moments, hunger eventually overcame Herr Josef and he started, as discreetly as he could, chewing into his dinner and filling the room with the smell of it all. Parviz's meditation had to stop.

Strange to remember that five years ago he wouldn't even have known or cared whether his prayer was Christian or Muslem. Even stranger to think he had adopted, or rather returned to, the religion of his jailers – if in a distinctly more moderate form. Christian prayer had not seemed to offer very much in the middle of that barren desert. Unless it was simply the spirit of the past, or past spirits, that had moved him in that abandoned caravanserei – the ghosts of the Bedouin stitching that early world together with their trade routes.

Tonight, once prayer was interrupted, he did not know

where to turn his thoughts. Sasan had bewildered him. He had talked in those brief moments at the crematorium as though he and Shaheenee were already under the aegis of some other group, country or individual on the outside. Veltri? But then they would know Veltri had been arrested. Unless there were others with Veltri. Sasan had also spoken of ten days – the next ten days. What could happen in ten days to change anyone's world?

Morgan had bailed out of McGovern's car outside the V & A. 'Museum's closed,' was McGovern's parting witticism. He'd walked to South Kensington, taken the Underground west again to Heathrow and a taxi to ride round the airport perimeter till he found the 'hostel'.

A dreary little prison it was, with a window in the outside door for the examination of ID cards; peeling paint and graffiti up the stairs inside; the doors numbered and double-locked like cells.

Dorff had finished sucking his chicken bones when he opened the door to Morgan's knock. 'We don't even have standing room in here, buddy.'

Morgan pushed past him into the room. 'Take a break,' he told Dorff. 'Buy yourself a beer.'

Dorff glanced at Parviz, then looked back at Morgan. 'You signing for him?'

'He won't run away.'

Still doubtful, Dorff picked up his coat, dropping the keys into Morgan's hand. Morgan closed and locked the door behind him as he went, then walked to the window. He could see Dorff downstairs at the entrance talking to the security goon, making sure Morgan wasn't going to abscond with his prisoner. Parviz, brittle and apprehensive, was on the bed behind him.

'Hardly usual for anyone from your country, whether Muslem or Christian, to be cremated, is it?' Morgan turned away from the window to face him. 'So who, I wonder, arranged cremation for Farshid Sabet?'

123

Parviz was watching him without offering a reply.

Morgan sat on the end of the bed, moving the plastic box with half-eaten chicken and chips. 'You won't be surprised if I tell you he was assassinated.'

Parviz closed his eyes and turned his head away. 'How?'

'A hypodermic up his nose. Insulin, probably. Highly professional. Would normally have been passed off as natural causes.' Morgan paused. He imagined interrogation would be counter-productive with Parviz. If he had the time, he'd have to move a little more gently. 'Would I be right in thinking they've been hunting your friends now for something like four years?'

'Five years,' replied Parviz.

'Five years. But now suddenly the urgency is such that they spirit you out of prison and make sure the newspapers spread the news of your whereabouts. Farshid Sabet comes out of hiding and is almost immediately killed. And rather foolishly to his funeral – to his cremation, his would-have-been cremation – comes Sasan Sasanee, who as a result will now be in mortal danger. You're being used as bait, Mr Vaziree.'

A plane landed outside, with a sudden blast of reverse thrust as it passed fifty yards or so away. Morgan looked up at the window. 'Doesn't sound as though you get much sleep in here.' Morgan took the noughts and crosses photograph from his pocket and laid it on the bed in front of Parviz. 'Who's the girl?'

Parviz stared at the photograph. Six years ago he'd seen it on the front page of every newspaper back home the day after his father had been shot.

'She was at the crematorium,' said Morgan.

'Ask your German friend,' replied Parviz.

'Oxford?'

Parviz was silent.

'Two nights ago you stayed in Oxford. If I remember the entry Mr Dorff made on your file, the name of your host was Ashley Buchanan.'

124

'He was at the embassy in Teheran ten years ago. A close friend of my father.'

'And the girl?'

'His daughter, Annabel.'

Morgan referred back to the photograph lying on the bed between them. 'At the time of his death, your father was said to have been a moderating influence. I take that to mean your father was more sympathetic to the Americans than he was to the Russians.' Morgan looked up at Parviz.

'If you know the answers, why ask the questions?'

'I don't know the answers. I'm asking you.'

'My father favoured neither Americans nor Russians. He told his people, he told me, that even if it meant waiting a thousand years we had to make our own future. He was a moderating influence only on those who sought revolution from the outside.'

'And that is why he was killed?' Morgan tapped the photograph with his finger. 'Six years ago your father was killed. What is happening now, or about to happen now, that makes people start to kill again?'

'Inside my country, the killing has never stopped.'

A rap on the door seemed to signal Dorff's return. Morgan lowered his voice, his question now urgent: 'What did Sasan say to you today that made you so angry?'

Parviz was silent. The rap at the door was repeated, louder this time.

'I'm trying to help you,' said Morgan.

An English voice outside called through the door. 'Mr Dorff?'

Morgan unlocked and opened the door. A young police motorcyclist was standing outside, an envelope in his hand. Morgan recognized the blue line across one corner.

'Mr Dorff?' the young policeman asked.

'Yes.' Morgan nodded, holding out his hand for the envelope.

'You are Mr Josef Dorff?'

'He'll be back in a minute.'

'I'll wait downstairs, sir.'

'That's from the Interpol office in Scotland Yard,' said Morgan, pointing at the envelope. 'I have an ID card.'

The young copper looked at him. 'Mr Dorff has to sign for it in person.' And he turned away to the stairs.

Morgan closed the door and looked back at Parviz, who was staring at the floor. 'I don't know who you are,' Parviz said, 'nor why you are trying to help me, but to me you remain a policeman and I will not trust even one of you.' He looked up at Morgan. 'If you have problems with your conscience, take it to your priest.'

Morgan walked past him to the window. Dorff had met the young police motor-cyclist at the hostel entrance; he tucked the beer cans under his chin while he signed for the envelope.

Morgan grabbed his bag and made for the door. 'Morgan's my name,' he said to Parviz. 'Unfortunately, I have no priest.'

He locked the door behind him, leaving the key on the outside, and turned away from the stairs as he heard Dorff coming up; he even heard Dorff swear to himself when he found the key in the door, not realizing that Morgan was still only yards away from him round the corner of the corridor.

Morgan's premonition was correct. Once back inside the room with Parviz, Dorff waved the envelope and enclosed telex at him. 'You won't be seeing any more of Hunter-Brown. He is officially withdrawn from the case.' Dorff chucked a can of beer at Parviz. 'I wonder how the foxy son of a bitch knew what was coming?'

Morgan jumped on a bus heading back into town. He'd remembered Laleh talking about a party on Thursday evening.

5

'I do not believe we have ever pretended to a monopoly either of wisdom or justice, young lady.' Blind Hugh was holding court, and Laleh eavesdropped as she walked to the kitchen. The Buchanan girl was in the dock, with a couple of the embassy heavyweights and an ex-Reagan speechwriter hovering at Hugh's shoulder. Ashley Buchanan had disappeared. Laleh collected empty plates, still tuned in across the room to Hugh's authoritative voice. 'Nor would we presume to impose any such monopoly on our major allies.'

The Buchanan girl was fighting her corner. 'But you do, unfortunately, have something of a monopoly of power – military and economic.' Ashley would have recognized warning lights flashing in Annie's eyes.

'Indeed so, young lady,' replied Hugh, his face turning to the direction of her voice. 'And in order to preserve our democratic freedoms, that power has sometimes to be exercised in ways not everyone agrees with. The major freedom, the larger freedom has to prevail.'

'God Bless America,' retorted Annie. Hugh detecting the sneer in her voice, guessed the expression on her face.

'The stable running of the British Empire,' he said, 'often met with exactly the same kind of problems and exactly the same suppressions of smaller national freedoms.'

'The British Empire,' Annie replied, 'fell on its fucking arse.'

Laleh moved into the kitchen. Time to find Cal, she thought, and have Hugh's little hit squad dispersed. She picked up a bowl of cream to carry back to the sitting room. There was a voice at her ear as she passed the stairs.

'Hey!' Roundie, with a grinning face, reached a spoon through the bannisters and scooped the cherry off the top of the cream.

'Roundie!'

'There's no law, Lal, against eating and being fat and happy.'

'There's a law of aesthetics,' laughed Laleh.

'I lost that race a long time ago' – Roundie nodded at the study door and Cal, his back turned, talking to someone '– to yon Cal with his lean and hungry look who stole my bride away.'

'You dated me once, Roundie. And took me for a hamburger in Central Park.'

'I was too busy. Too dedicated to my work.'

Laleh laughed again. 'As I recall, you wanted me to be your mole at the United Nations.' Laleh stopped, and took a pace back to see who Cal was talking to. Ashley Buchanan. And they were very deep in confabulation.

Roundie watched her. 'Conspirators?' he asked. His tone of voice made Laleh turn to look at him, but her intended question was diverted by the sudden and brusque exit of Annabel Buchanan from the sitting room to pick up her coat and storm out of the front door without a backward glance.

Morgan was twenty yards along the street when he heard the door slam. He'd been taking car numbers up and down the road. Most of the cars had CD plates, and one or two had waiting drivers.

He recognized Annie as she came out of the gate, and walked up behind her as she was trying to unlock the door of her battered yellow Renault.

'Party over?'

She hadn't heard his approach and looked round as though someone had stuck a gun in her back. Then almost instantly recognized him. 'You were at the crematorium this afternoon,' she said.

Morgan pulled the noughts and crosses photograph from a pocket and shone his pencil–beam torch at it. 'Not many of them left, are there?'

'Who are you?'

'Perhaps you heard what Sasan and Parviz were saying to each other this afternoon? What it was that made Parviz so angry?'

Annie stared at him. 'I heard nothing.'

Morgan pointed the torch and a finger at Annie's own face on the photograph. 'Annabel Buchanan,' he said.

'Are you a cop?'

'A few seconds after that picture was taken the old man was shot.'

'Who the hell are you?'

'I'm a researcher for Interpol.'

'What does that make you?'

'Powerless, so far as I know.'

'But I have to answer your questions!'

Morgan shook his head.

Annie opened the door of her car, climbed in and slammed it shut.

Left on his own for the first time that week, Jasper had enjoyed a very peaceful and frugal evening: one tin of sardines, two slices of dry toast and a glass of sherry. 'Home at midnight, Jasper,' Ashley had said. But no hint from either of them as to when they'd be returning north to their real home. Nice though it was to have company and large though the house was, it remained an imposition. Like fish, guests tend to make their presence felt after more than a few days.

Jasper was trying to cope unsuccessfully with a rather

brash translation of Homer by some Canadian poet. The review had to be posted by the weekend and he could not for the life of him think of anything original to say. He'd have to dig out one of his old lectures: talk about Homer and not the merits of translation and footnotes.

He'd also, he realized, sipped rather too much claret in college at lunch-time. The SCR steward was altogether too swift on the refill. One tended to lose count. His head kept nodding forward and jerking back as he dozed and awoke in fits and starts, totally unaware he was being watched through the uncurtained window at the end of the room.

6

Morgan climbed steps out of the Underground into the late evening crowds, Mack the Knife running somewhere in his head. 'A great fire in Soho', and 'Komm heraus, du Schönheit von Soho'. But most of Soho's beauties these days were far too young.

Morgan walked round a corner where he could remember girls lining up two deep at five in the afternoon. 'Das ist ihr Mädchen, Herr Jakob Schmidt.' And would you, Morgan, pay for one tonight?

The police motorbike was pulled up on its stand outside Rudi's door. Morgan walked straight past without a sideways glance, round two corners and back on his tracks.

'Are you alone?' he asked his brother over the only pay-phone in Wardour Street still working.

'No,' was Rudi's guarded reply.

'Is he delivering?'

'Yes.'

'I have to sign for it?'

'Yes.'

'An envelope with blue lines?'

'Yes.'

Morgan smiled. 'Is he watching you?'

Rudi laughed down the phone, 'Yes.'

'See you some time, little brother.'

'Are you in town?'

Morgan looked out at a bus crossing the lights on Shaftesbury Avenue. 'I'll find somewhere to sleep. Best not to tell you in case he starts pulling your finger-nails out.'

'Damn right.'

Morgan grinned to himself again. 'Do you see the moon over Soho?'

'*Ich seh' ihn, Lieber. Ich seh' ihn.*'

'He's a pretty boy in that uniform, isn't he?' Morgan imagined the young policeman in his leather boots sitting at Rudi's kitchen table, and Rudi turning to look at him.

'Lovely,' came Rudi's voice, camping it up.

'You behave yourself, little brother. Policemen have stings in their tails.'

Morgan bought a bottle of wine at French's with ten minutes to spare and walked across half his childhood kingdom, down into the decaying mews where Beth kept her barrow chained to the wall. He was surprised she even answered the door at this time of night.

'You, is it, ducky,' she cackled through the crack of the door. 'Running away from Old Bill, are you?'

'Something like that, Beth.'

He heard her pull bolts on the door like a medieval castle's. 'If your mother could see you now,' she said as she opened up for him.

Morgan held out the bottle of wine.

'Board and lodging, ducky?'

Morgan nodded.

'Cost you a game of cards.'

'If you say so.'

She bolted up the door again and led him past crates of fruit and veg to the stairs. 'You'll have to sleep with the cabbages.' She cackled a laugh. 'Unless you want to sleep with me.'

Jasper had no idea what the time was when he woke. The room was strangely cold, as though a door or

132

window were open somewhere. He thought a noise had woken him. Perhaps the front door.

'Is that you, Ashley?'

There was no reply, yet Jasper was quite sure someone was in the house. Perhaps Ashley and Annie were back and in the kitchen making cocoa. Yes, a mug of hot chocolate would be nice. Jasper looked down at the book that had slipped from his lap onto his knees. But then began to doze again.

The face behind him did not move; hardly seemed to breathe, until Jasper was sleeping again.

An Arab face Farshid and Sasan would have recognized as the last they'd ever seen.

7

It was half past midnight before the house was clear, the ambassador's handmaidens chauffered home and only the boxes of washed and dried glasses left behind for an embassy car to pick up in the morning.

'Never again,' said Laleh in the kitchen. 'They can have takeaways from McDonalds next time.'

Roundie was grinning at her across the kitchen table; Cal was sipping whisky, silent in the third chair, abstracted.

'Are we contemplating a drunken night?' Roundie asked.

'I'm contemplating my bed,' replied Laleh.

'And Cal his navel.' Roundie topped up his glass. 'Anyone figure out why the pretty English girl left in such a huff?'

'Blind Hugh pontificating,' said Laleh.

'So was she when I last heard her.' Roundie drew patterns in the air with a finger. 'Rather to the left, I thought she was.'

Laleh laughed, conscious of Cal's continued silence next to her. 'Go and play a lullaby, Roundie.'

Roundie heaved himself off his chair. 'Something full of *Ausschmückung*?'

Laleh waited until she heard Roundie at the piano in the sitting room.

'You're very silent,' she said to her husband.

'It's a curious business, isn't it.'

'What is curious?'

134

'Sudden moves on the diplomatic front just because a political refugee is given a few days' furlough.'

'You seem to know more about it all than I do.'

'I was given the file at the embassy today.'

'You?'

'It seems I'm meant to be talking with this Parviz whatever-his-name-is.'

'Vaziree.'

'I'm on Concorde tomorrow for a briefing in Washington.'

'Why you?'

'I suppose through my wife I'm meant to know more about the subject than any of the others.'

'You mean I've been spying for you?'

'I didn't say that, Lal.'

'I've been working with these people for four days and today you are given the file, completely out of the blue?'

Laleh could hear Roundie's 'Clair de Lune' dying away as, doubtless, he strained to hear their sounds of disagreement. He loved to act as peacemaker. Laleh lowered her voice. 'I just don't believe, Cal, you knew nothing about it before today.'

'Sometimes they understand very little, the Americans.'

Annie looked round. Her father's face was only visible in outline from the dashboard light. She thought he'd been asleep since High Wycombe.

'This will be another game they'll lose to the Russians,' he went on. 'Without even realizing the game is being played.'

Annie looked round again. 'The Russians?' You old fox, she thought. What are you up to now? Letting me know you know? Or trying to lull me with false optimism?

They were over the top of the Chilterns, half an hour

from home. An hour and a half late, if Uncle Jasper was counting.

Jasper was dead to the world in his armchair, aware, every now and then of noises in the house but not enough to be alarmed, subconsciously still waiting for a mug of cocoa.

The surviving red rose on the bedside table in the boxroom upstairs shed another petal as the gloved hands eased open the drawer in their careful and methodical search. Each room had been toothcombed but everything left as found, without signs of search or intrusion.

The Arab returned downstairs and into the sitting room, where the old man was sleeping. Bookshelves, writing desk, the drawers of an old bureau: he eventually found what he was looking for in an old black leather bag, monogrammed with a rather faded *E II R* – three letters from three separate oil companies, addressed to 'Dear Mr Buchanan', 'Dear Buchanan', and 'Dear Ashley'. The Arab began laboriously to copy the texts.

He was only halfway through the first letter when he heard the car on the road outside and saw headlights turn across the windows. Behind him the old man stirred in his chair. 'Is that you, Ashley?' The Arab picked up a heavy paperweight and turned towards the egg-like skull under the standard lamp.

Annie had been quite surprised to see lights still on in the sitting room. 'Uncle Jasper, we're back!' she called.

Ashley, who'd been snoozing in the car, looked a bit bleary, but both of them heard the sound of something, or someone, in the scullery or kitchen. 'Jasper?'

Annie pushed open the door of the sitting room. Jasper was slumped in his chair, book at his feet, head on his chest. 'Uncle J?'

Annie knelt by the chair.

136

Outside, the Arab was running lightly round the house, slowing to a walk as he used a side gate onto the road.

Ashley touched his brother on the shoulder. 'Are you all right, Jasper?'

The eggshell skull moved and the turtle-like eyes blinked open, looking round at brother and niece. 'Oh dear, must have dozed off.' Jasper actually smiled for the first time in seven days. 'Isn't that cocoa ready yet?'

8

The maid pushed the breakfast trolley up the hotel corridor and knocked at room number 212.

'*Avanti!* Come in,' came the muffled voice from inside.

A man stepped from a service door at the maid's shoulder, pressed a pound note in her hand and took the trolley from her with a wink and a grin. 'Friend of the family,' he said, and pushed the room door open.

Roberto Assuntino had lived six years of his professional life under the threat of terrorism. He had witnessed the shooting of his closest colleague, investigated the assassinations of two others, and finally himself been kneecapped by two young students, a long-haired youth on a motorbike and a beautiful girl riding pillion. It had been the beautiful girl who had pulled out the gun.

Not surprising now, as he walked from the bathroom, drying his hair, and saw the strange man in his room, if he was a little frightened. He picked up a bottle of mineral water from the table and raised it as a weapon. '*Come si permette?*' he shouted.

Even the grinning Roundie looked alarmed for a moment. 'I'm not a terrorist, Mr Assuntino. I'm a journalist. *Giornalista Americano,*' he added in his awful Italian.

'*Non ho la minima intenzione di parlare –* '

'I'm not here to ask questions, Mr Assuntino. I'm here to offer you evidence that would incriminate Mr Veltri.' Roundie tapped the bag he was carrying.

Assuntino still held the bottle raised against him. '*Ha

138

una tessera? You have a card?' And as Roundie slipped a hand inside his anorak, 'Slowly,' he shouted.

This Italian is really very frightened, thought Roundie. He held his jerkin open to show the card before he pulled it from his jacket.

'Ralph Curtiss, Panmeridian Press,' the Italian read aloud off the card.

'My agency,' said Roundie. 'I'm a freelance working through them. I've been chasing this story for six months now.'

'Story?'

'Mr Veltri and armaments?'

Only now was the bottle lowered.

'I have documentation,' said Roundie, 'that proves Mr Veltri was arranging the passage of Exocet missiles from France to Argentina through South Africa during the Falklands War.' Again moving slowly not to alarm the *magistrato*, Roundie opened his briefcase and took out a piece of paper. 'Mr Veltri's share of the transaction was paid in advance into this bank account in London.'

Assuntino set the bottle back on the table, took his dressing-gown off the bed and pulled it on.

Roundie went on: 'I imagine if the British authorities knew of these documents, they would be most reluctant to grant extradition. Mr Veltri would be tried for the arms crime in this country and would spend, I think, six or seven very uncushioned years in an English prison.' Roundie tapped his briefcase. 'If Mr Veltri knew of the existence of these documents, I think he'd be wanting to get the hell out of the UK as fast as possible. I imagine he would choose to return home and take his chances there with you.'

'I can see these documents?' Assuntino reached a hand to Roundie's briefcase.

'I'll give you photocopies of the two telex orders that originated the deal. Mr Veltri would recognize them very quickly.'

Assuntino took the photocopies and read them. 'And if

139

I tell the English authorities you have these documents?'

'I would lose a good story. But you would lose your prisoner.'

'Why you' – Assuntino paused, searching for the word ' – volunteer this to me?'

'*Sub judice*,' replied Roundie. 'While Mr Veltri is held under British law, I can't use my story. There's six months of my life tied up in it. What you might call a substantial investment.'

Assuntino waved Roundie to the armchair.

Roundie was watching the Italian. 'I think if you remind Mr Veltri about selling Exocets to Argentina, he'll suddenly find he has no more reason to contest extradition from the United Kingdom.' Roundie grinned. 'This conversation, of course, has never taken place.' Roundie lifted the cover off Assuntino's eggs and bacon. It smelt very good. 'You're not going to eat all of this yourself, are you?'

9

Morgan woke up to the smell of cauliflower and the sounds of Beth loading her barrow in the yard outside, fingerless mittens humping boxes Morgan knew he'd never have been able to lift – Beth, who returned from the war in Spain at the age of eighteen, the fighting mascot of a dozen Durham miners from the XVth.

Talk to Beth about it now and she'd pretend she remembered nothing. But it was all buried deep in Morgan's emotional fabric – Papa's leg of Parma ham hurled at the official from the Italian Embassy who entered the shop one day flourishing the Fascist salute; mother's pyramid of Chianti bottles collapsing like a house of cards around him as he fell; and the bully-boys from embassy or consulate who came the next night to wreck the shop or worse, Beth with her dozen miners, ten hours off the boat-train from Spain, chasing the blackshirts up Dean Street – and, inevitably, invited by Papa into that den of kitchens behind the shop for *grappa* and *panforte*. For seven or eight years afterwards, most of that dozen trekked south once a year on the anniversary, invited by Papa, to a meal and a crate of wine in that same kitchen, the sounds of singing leaking out into Old Compton Street over air-raid sirens or the sidling mutters of the black-market spivs – 'There's a place in Spain called Jarama', to the tune of 'Red River Valley'.

Beth shouted a goodbye from the yard and Morgan listened to the wooden wheels trundling up the mews. She wouldn't have let him help if he'd tried. Just as well she didn't know what was hidden in a plastic bag under one of her crates of grapes.

Morgan left ten minutes later, down Old Compton Street for a coffee at Valerie's, watching the door for Rudi in the street outside, and watching his watch for the 9.10 train ten minutes away in a taxi. Rudi walked in at ten to nine with an armful of newspapers and a sheepish grin. The lorry driver was back from Budapest.

Morgan boarded the train with a minute and a half to spare and saw Laleh watching him down the aisle of the dining-car. Cool and detached, he thought, and wouldn't have expected otherwise after their scratch at the crematorium yesterday afternoon. But her coolness was also hiding a little surprise – Josef Dorff in the seat opposite her, turning round as Morgan reached the table.

'Gotcha!'

Morgan looked round at the table behind him and the tables beyond. 'Lost Mr Vaziree?'

'He's safe enough, Joe. With your English bobbies in that god-awful police wagon. I thought I'd try to save you the journey.' He pulled the blue striped envelope from his pocket. 'Sorry, buddy-boy. Your credentials are withdrawn.'

'What credentials?' asked Laleh across the table. She was looking a little bewildered.

'He's off the case, lady,' explained Dorff and looked back at Morgan. 'I get the file, and you can take a holiday.'

Morgan pulled the telex out of the envelope, read it and looked at Dorff. 'No department code and no reference numbers? You must admit, "Buddy-boy", any damn fool can send a telex.'

Dorff nodded at Morgan's black bag. 'The red file, Joe.'

Morgan dropped the bag on to the seat beside Dorff and watched him zip it open. A couple of dirty shirts, four pairs of socks and a toilet bag was all he found.

'I was given the file by Elgin,' said Morgan. 'It stays with me until Elgin, personally, takes it off me.'

'You're committing an offence, Joe.'

'An administrative offence.' Morgan retrieved his bag and nodded at Laleh. 'Goodbye, Mrs Colraine.' He turned away. Whistles were blowing on the platform outside. He stepped off the train as it moved, walking back up the ramp reading and re-reading the telegram.

He rang Paris from the card-phone on the station. Elgin was unavailable – 'out of Paris'.

'Still running away, ducky?' asked Beth when he burrowed under her stall in Berwick Street market. He pulled out the plastic bag with his red file and winked at her.

'You look unhappy,' she said.

'Maybe I've fallen in love, Beth.'

He stayed with her the rest of the morning, selling cauliflowers and grapes and trying to make up his mind what to do.

10

'Mr Morgan is off the case,' Parviz told Laleh when she walked into their prison office that morning.

She nodded. 'I know.'

Parviz glanced at Dorff. 'Perhaps he was doing his job too well.'

Dorff looked round at him.

All three of them were in the outer office watching the *magistrato* with Veltri and his solicitor in the inner room. Whatever the *magistrato* had said to Veltri and whatever the two documents he had handed to him, they had silenced the voluble Italian. Already prison-pale, he seemed to have turned a few shades greyer still. He huddled with his solicitor as Assuntino called the others in, to sit at their by now habitual places round the table.

Veltri's solicitor stood up. 'I believe these proceedings might be redundant. Given two conditions, my client will no longer contest extradition and is willing to return without delay to Italy.'

Laleh was translating word for word in a murmur for the *magistrato*. He in turn put his own question for Laleh to translate.

'What conditions?' Laleh asked the solicitor.

'That until the time of his trial in Italy, he is held under house arrest and not in prison. And that he is allowed his own bodyguards for his protection.'

Assuntino looked down the table at Veltri. '*Al confino allora.*'

Veltri did not respond.

'What the hell is "*confino*",' asked Dorff.

Veltri himself replied. 'Exile. Usually to a very small and cold village high in the mountains and as far away from your own home as possible. As a form of confinement it dates back to the times of ancient Rome. You are free to do whatever you like in the village. Except leave.'

'What's the matter with here?' asked Dorff. 'You don't like English prison?'

Assuntino was murmuring with Laleh. She translated the murmur to the table at large: 'Mr Veltri's decision will mean the transfer of the whole investigation to Italy.'

There was a short silence. 'Is there no one left to kill in England?' asked Parviz.

'What's that meant to mean, Garibaldi?'

Parviz looked across the table at Laleh. 'What if I refuse to go to Italy?'

'You have no choice, Garibaldi.' Again the aggressive Dorff.

Parviz was still looking at Laleh. 'Will *you* be coming to Italy?'

The *magistrato* smiled. 'We have our own interpreters in Italy.'

'I ask for someone *I* can trust,' said Parviz.

Laleh stared at Parviz.

Dorff sneered. 'And who pays her?'

'I pay,' replied Parviz.

'What with? Chick-peas?'

Laleh was still looking at Parviz. 'I will lend him the money to pay me,' she said.

Laleh was home by quarter past three that afternoon, the silence of the house oppressive and her own thoughts very confused. She would have liked Morgan there to ask questions or answer hers.

She walked through to the kitchen and saw Cal's

message on the board. '*Gone to Washington, back tomorrow – Cal.*'

'*Going to Italy*,' Laleh scribbled underneath, '*back next week.*'

She saw another scribble on the board and remembered Morgan leaving the telephone number and address of his brother in Soho. At least she could tell him what had happened in Birmingham that morning.

The telephone rang in Rudi's blitzed-out room. The German ignoring it. He was very thorough in his search and had no intention, it seemed, of hiding his visit in any way.

Dorff left empty-handed, unaware of the next pair of 'visitors' waiting for him to go. The two Arabs were seen climbing the rickety stairs by 'oral French' at a quarter past four that afternoon. Ten minutes later Laleh arrived by taxi at the end of the alley and asked the driver to wait.

Once she'd found the door, she climbed those same rickety stairs to the very top and knocked on the door marked *Giugiardini*. The door was slightly ajar and she noticed the wood splintered round the lock.

'Is there anyone there?' she called out, and pushed the door further open, alarmed at what she then saw: drawers and cupboards had been emptied, the bed was lying on its side, clothes were scattered on the floor. Laleh had an envelope in her hand – a note for Morgan to tell him the investigation was moving to Italy, and Parviz with it. It was difficult to see where to leave the envelope in all that mess. She propped it on the telephone.

As she turned back towards the door she was aware of shadows moving behind and above her. She looked up. Two faces were watching her through the skylight – two Arab faces – the same two faces that had passed her at the ticket barrier on the station the day before.

146

Recognition and alarm were mutual: the killer kicked in the glass of the skylight as Laleh fled through the door and down the stairs.

She heard the thud as both of them dropped into the room and another crash as the killer jumped the first flight of stairs behind her. There was suddenly no doubt in her mind that if he caught her he *would* kill her.

A voice called out from one of the other rooms, a girl's voice, in some alarm. Laleh reached the street door as the killer turned the last flight behind her. Again he jumped, but as she slammed the door shut so the latch must have sprung and the delay, no more than a second or two, was enough to see her to the end of the alley and the safety of the Wardour Street pavements. She fell back into her waiting taxi.

The driver turned his head in some surprise. 'Where to, lady?'

'Anywhere – just drive.' She flicked the window lock on both doors and prayed the lights would stay green on Shaftesbury Avenue; then she looked round through the back window and saw the two Arabs running from the alley, one of them holding the letter she had left for Morgan.

'North, south, east or west?' called the driver as the lights turned to amber in front of them.

'West,' she said and he turned towards Piccadilly. The two Arabs abandoned pursuit.

The taxi driver was watching her in the mirror.

'Could you take me to Twyford?' she asked.

11

'Stationmaster's gone home already,' said the young porter. 'He was up most of last night. We had an accident here yesterday.'

'They said someone fell under a train.'

'Threw himself, more likely.'

'Does anyone know who it was?'

The porter nodded through the gate at the newspaper stand. 'Photograph's in the local paper, miss. An Italian.'

'Italian?' Laleh lifted the lid of the newspaper stand. A small photograph at the foot of the front page told her what she had already feared.

'Sod's law,' laughed Rudi as he heard his telephone ringing from the bottom of the stairs. 'If I run for it, it'll stop just before I pick it up.'

Rudi had been busking when Morgan found him. Playing Debussy to the rush-hour crowds making for Charing Cross. 'Come to say goodbye?' he'd asked.

Now he was running up the stairs for the telephone, but stopped short when he saw his door ajar. Neither he nor Morgan could quite believe what they found when they walked in.

Rudi looked up at the broken skylight. 'Didn't mess about, did they?' He picked up the phone.

McGovern or Dorff, Morgan was asking himself as he surveyed the damage to his brother's flat.

'A Mrs Colraine?' said Rudi holding out the phone. 'From a call-box.'

Morgan almost snatched it from his hand.

'Sasan's dead,' he heard her say. 'He fell under a train at Twyford Station. I think they killed him.' Her voice was flat and shocked.

'They? They who?'

'They were there at your brother's flat. I saw them.' The pips went.

'Where are you?' called Morgan.

'I'm here on the station. Twyford.'

'Wait there for me,' said Morgan in the split second before the phone cut off.

Morgan turned round as he put the phone down. Rudi was on his knees picking up pieces of glass from the broken skylight. 'Do you have somewhere you can go tonight?' Morgan asked him.

'And let the rats and the rain walk in here?'

'Is there anyone who can help you fix it?'

Rudi stood up and surveyed the wreckage of his little flat. 'Is this McGovern?'

Morgan shook his head. 'No.'

Rudi almost laughed. 'You mean there's someone worse than McGovern?'

Morgan squatted down to pick up a book. 'I'm sorry, Rudi.'

'Sod off. You have things to do.'

Morgan stood up. 'Will money help?'

'Just sodding off will help.'

Morgan made Paddington in twelve minutes on the Bakerloo, left a message for McGovern from a pay-phone on the station and jumped the first 125 heading out to Reading. He did look for Laleh as they tore through Twyford – but the platforms seemed empty.

By the time a taxi had ferried him back from Reading the sun was going down, the evening's commuters almost all safely home.

Laleh was sitting on a bench across the station, the side Morgan had not been looking when his own train passed through. She saw him as he turned up the steps of the footbridge, and they met halfway across the bridge. Laleh pushed a copy of the local newspaper into Morgan's hand.

'Sasan was on the bench where I was sitting,' she said. 'Apparently there were two men on the platform with him. I saw two men leave the station yesterday half a minute after it all happened. I saw the same two men at your brother's flat today.'

'My brother's flat? What were you doing there?'

'I came to leave you a note. I wanted you to know that Veltri has decided to go back.'

'To Italy?'

'He's no longer contesting extradition. They're taking Parviz out there to continue the investigation. Parviz has asked me to go as well. He seems very frightened.'

Her last words were almost obliterated as a 125 roared through the station under their feet. Laleh put a hand to her head against the noise, and Morgan touched her shoulder as they waited for the noise to subside.

'I'd say Mr Parviz Vaziree has good reason to be frightened,' said Morgan. He turned Laleh back to the stairs. 'Now will you tell me what it was Sasan said in the crematorium that made Parviz so angry?'

'It wasn't clear,' replied Laleh. 'They kept interrupting each other and switching languages. I think Sasan was worried too many of us could understand what they were saying. He told Parviz to spin things out as long as he could – get sick, anything – because in two weeks' time it could all be over. It was life or death – those were his words.'

Two weeks?

'That's when Parviz got angry. He said there must be

no foreign intervention. He said: "I would rather die than face another slavery."'

Morgan could see two police cars in the forecourt outside. He stopped and turned to Laleh. 'Those two men at my brother's place – did they see you?'

Laleh nodded.

'They recognized you?'

Laleh nodded again.

Morgan watched McGovern and Pike following the local uniformed mob up the stairs, and the porter escorting a little old lady with them.

'Don't say I didn't call you this time,' said Morgan, and pushed the newspaper with Sasan's photograph into McGovern's hand.

'One day,' replied McGovern, 'you'll let me decide for myself whether or not it's homicide.'

'Only Italian Freemasons hang themselves from bridges or fall unaided under trains.'

McGovern stopped on the stairs. 'What's that meant to mean?'

'Calvi,' replied Morgan over his shoulder as he trotted on down the stairs. 'Hung himself on scaffolding under Blackfriars Bridge as the tide was coming in – or so you chaps claimed. He'd even put bricks down his trousers. To help keep his balance, I suppose.' Morgan turned at the foot of the steps. 'Surely you Special Branch chaps were called in to give your expert advice. I mean, most of you are Freemasons, aren't you.'

'You both stay where I can find you!' McGovern's angry shout was to be his farewell to them both. 'If you go anywhere, I want to know where.'

Morgan and Laleh walked out into the forecourt. 'Where *are* you going?' she asked him.

'Wherever you're going,' replied Morgan.

Laleh's patient cab-driver was still waiting for her. 'North, south, east or west?' he asked her through his open window.

Laleh turned to Morgan. 'Where *should* I be going?'

'Home for your bags.'

'And then?'

'Paris.'

'Why Paris?'

'It's on the way to Italy. And we keep faces on file there. You might identify your two Arabs.'

They were both looking through the station fence across the four tracks at the group on the far platform: McGovern and Pike, the uniformed boys, the porter and the little old lady who was moving them around like a fussy film director with actors on a set. McGovern somehow ended up playing the part of Sasan, propelled by Pike and a uniform towards the edge of the platform, until he broke away from them, belabouring them both with the newspaper Morgan had handed him.

12

The thin beam of light from a pocket torch moved round the bedroom, across the dressing-table and onto the small silver frame. Two hands propped the torch against the mirror and unfastened the frame to sift through the photographs packed inside, the same middle-aged man in each photograph, wearing round metal-frame glasses and either holding or smoking a pipe: a broken white wall somewhere in Andalucia; a little girl in a Roman street and on a Tuscan farm – '*Val d'Orcia*' scrawled on the back of the picture. A railway ticket from Pisa to Port Bou. A father and a mother and a daughter.

A taxi pulled up in the road outside, its noisy engine ticking over. The two hands carefully reassembled the frame and switched off the torch. The curtains were open. A murmur of voices and a short laugh came from the street. 'I could pay you in Swiss Francs,' said a man's voice.

The intruder walked to the bedroom window and watched Laleh under the street-lamps outside writing a cheque on the roof of the cab. Whoever was watching moved quietly in the darkness out of the bedroom and down the landing to the head of the stairs.

'There's brandy somewhere,' said Laleh as she opened the front door. 'I think I need its medicinal effect.' She led Morgan into the sitting room, turned on the light and closed the curtains. A floorboard creaked upstairs as the intruder withdrew across the landing to use the spiral stairs at the back of the house. Morgan looked up at the ceiling.

'Don't worry,' said Laleh. 'It's an old house. It creaks and groans sometimes.' She poured two brandies, handed one to Morgan and shivered. 'It's cold.'

They were standing close, looking at each other. Morgan reached out a hand to touch her face. Laleh took a step forward into his arms, her head down on his shoulder, a hand round the back of his head.

'Hold me,' she whispered, and turned her face towards his mouth.

Then froze suddenly like a block of stone staring over his shoulder at the pair of eyes and hooded head watching them through the partition.

PART FOUR

'Night Train'

1

Morgan saw terror in Laleh's eyes and sensed movement behind him. He spun her round to shield her and pushed her down onto the sofa and threw himself onto the floor. Then he looked up, feeling foolish as the main light was switched on and Roundie walked in.

'Cal gave me a key, Lal. Told me to look after you while he was gone.' Roundie was wrapped in a bathrobe, the hood of the bath robe over his head. 'I saw your message in the kitchen about going to Italy, and I thought you'd already gone.'

Laleh and Morgan both picked themselves up. Roundie grinned at them. 'The bodyguard, if I'm not mistaken. Looking after you all right, is he?' Roundie turned to the piano and ran two chords. 'Making whoopee,' he sang.

'Someone else has been killed, Roundie,' said Laleh.

'You didn't choose an easy job, did you?'

'I'm not sure that I did choose it.'

Roundie crossed the room, holding out his hand to Morgan. 'My name's Ralph Curtiss. Friend of the family.'

'Morgan Hunter-Brown,' replied Morgan.

'It's rude to stare, Lal,' laughed Roundie. 'I can't help it if your husband has exotic taste in bathrobes.'

Laleh turned away. 'I'll pack my bag,' she said to Morgan, and walked to the stairs, leaving the two men face to face across the sitting room.

Roundie grinned again at Morgan and looked at his

watch. 'Where could you be off to, I ask myself. There are no flights to Italy at this time of night.'

They both sat down opposite each other. 'Don't worry about a taxi,' said Roundie. 'I'll run you to the airport myself. I love driving at night.'

'We were thinking of eating first,' said Morgan.

Roundie grinned again. 'I love eating.'

Morgan watched him for a moment. 'I didn't see a car in the drive.'

'I can't find reverse on the damn thing. It has to stay in the street.' Roundie laughed yet again, still watching Morgan. 'Who's the dead man?' he asked.

Morgan didn't reply.

'Did the dead man have a name?'

'I expect so.' A longer silence now between them.

Roundie pointed a finger at himself. 'You've seen me in front of that jail in Birmingham – right?'

Morgan nodded. 'Right.'

'I've been working on this story for six months. Winson Green prison is the last of a great many places I've visited.'

'You're a journalist?'

Roundie stood up and walked to the piano, the grin and the smile both fading. 'Knock it off, Mr Hunter-Brown. You had me checked out two days ago. Panmeridian Press with a beige Metro on hire. I'll show you my press card when I get my clothes on. The agency's an agency – no more, no less. Moneywise it's as bad as being freelance. Or as good. Which is why I have no intention of losing this story.' Roundie looked up – Laleh was standing in the door. He took his hands off the keyboard and raised them above his head. 'Confession, Lal. I even took pictures of *you* at the prison.'

Laleh was staring at him. 'When did you find out I was working there?'

'When I saw you walk out the prison gate Monday afternoon.'

'But you came here that evening. Why didn't you say you'd seen me?'

'Because either you or Cal would have thrown me out. With good reason. I was keyholing you, Lal. Now I'm apologizing.'

'And you didn't want Cal to know you're working on this story?'

'While I was spying on you, no.'

'*Does* he know?'

'I wouldn't know with any precision what Cal does or does not know.' Roundie stood up from the piano. 'I guess your taxi-driver better get himself dressed.' The grin was back on his face, infectious as ever. 'I know somewhere nice to eat. It's quite a fun place. Serves you breakfast if you stay long enough.' He walked out.

Morgan listened to his measured tread up the stairs, then looked round at Laleh. 'I hadn't anticipated a fun place.'

'Roundie's a fun person, I'm afraid.' She paused. 'And an old friend.'

'An old friend who keeps secrets.'

'I expect he'd call them professional secrets.' Laleh walked to the door. 'I do trust him, Morgan. I always have.'

Morgan waited a few moments then followed her out into the hall. He could just hear their voices upstairs.

'Is Cal mixed up in this story?' Laleh was asking.

'Cal's not a newsman.'

'That wasn't my question.'

'I go where a story takes me, you know how it is.'

'And that isn't an answer. You don't trust Cal, do you?'

'Come on, Lal – him and me, we're buddies.'

'But would you say you really knew him?'

Morgan heard Roundie's pitch of voice change as though he'd cocked his chin up to tie his tie. 'What's that supposed to mean?'

'I don't know. It's just a question I've started asking myself.'

There was silence for a moment, then Roundie's voice came from the landing: 'Cal's a diplomat, darling. They hide themselves. It's an occupational disease.'

'Is that all he is? Just a diplomat?'

There was a laugh in Roundie's voice as he answered, as though trying to reassure her. 'Shit, Lal. I don't know.'

Morgan moved away from the foot of the stairs.

2

Ashley and Jasper were dining in college that evening – standard Friday protocol whenever Ashley was staying in Oxford.

He'd noticed Lennox eyeing him across the Common Room over sherry, and when they crossed the quad to hall Lennox actually volunteered information in conspiratorial undertone: 'Parviz Vaziree leaves the country tomorrow.' The old reptile must have been keeping tabs on his ex-pupil – unless of course Home Office themselves had been priming or pumping him. Unfortunately, Lennox had no idea *where* Parviz was being taken but did offer to make another telephone call. He knew the direct-line number of the computer room at Immigration and enough of the jargon to make himself sound official.

Perhaps Lennox was beginning to feel nostalgia for the cloak and dagger.

Poor Jasper had given up even trying to understand what was going on. He watched his brother slip out with Lennox between port and coffee. It seemed to Jasper that the whole world was conspiring in the most unlikely combinations.

Lennox's room was very bare and cold, perhaps to discourage his pupils from overstaying their welcome after tutorials. 'Who shall I pretend to be?' he asked Ashley as he picked up the phone.

'Cabinet Office?'

'Good heavens – that'd be treason.'

'How about Interpol?'

'Where would I be calling from?'

'Paris. Tell them you have documentation for Parviz's escort. He's German. His name's Dorff. You might be asking what flight they're leaving on.'

Lennox looked at Ashley and shook his head. 'Frightening how naturally deception comes to you.'

A minute and a half later they had the answer, read off the computer to Lennox: Parviz Vaziree and Josef Dorff were booked on a British Caledonian flight to Genoa tomorrow morning.

Left to herself that evening, Annie had made her own contact again, walking round the corner to the phone-box up the Banbury Road. As always, method of contact was Byzantine – she had to visit three different pay-phones before finally making a connection. And, as usual, communication was monosyllabic. She sometimes had difficulty believing there was anyone out there listening.

3

Roundie, as threatened, danced all night, mostly with Laleh, but occasionally, as she flagged, turning to one of the bright young things adorning the other tables. He was very good at making people laugh. He even made Morgan laugh, when Morgan wasn't thinking of the shambles he'd left Rudi with in the Soho flat.

At around four in the morning, Roundie winked at him and suggested they both threw credit cards in the plate with the bill for food and drink – mostly Roundie's food and drink. Morgan walked out cold-sober and hungry, a hundred pounds poorer, into early morning Mayfair, Roundie still laughing arm in arm with Laleh behind him. Morgan wondered if his agency paid him expenses.

Ralph Curtiss was still laughing when he drove his beige Metro into Heathrow as dawn was breaking, but even then was not content to drop them at the departures door. He parked his car and walked with them into Terminal One, standing at the desk while they bought tickets, and to the check-in while they were processed onto the first Paris flight of the morning.

'The one great disadvantage of flying,' said Morgan as Roundie finally left them at passport control, 'is once you're on an aeroplane everyone knows exactly where you're going to get off.'

Laleh smiled at him as they walked up the boarding ramp to the gate and watched the sunrise through the

163

windows. 'I'm sorry,' she said. About Roundie and 'fun' and a sleepless night, she meant.

Parviz heard their plane take off from his hostel cell on the airport perimeter without, of course, knowing they were on board. He was thinking about his own flight later in the day south to Italy, and wondering if Italy had not been the natural and chosen refuge for Sasan and Shaheenee – with Veltri's help. His thoughts during prayer that morning were for their safety.

'Fold your blankets, Garibaldi,' said the German. 'This was British hospitality.' Dorff was already washed and shaved, the blankets stacked neatly on his own bed.

McGovern knocked them up an hour later. 'When's your plane?' he asked Dorff, and chucked a green passport on the bed beside Parviz. 'Your prisoner has another body to identify. What's left of it.'

Parviz opened the passport, though there seemed no real need. An Italian passport, a face staring out at him. Sasan was dead.

4

Veltri and Assuntino had travelled that same early morning by small executive jet from Birmingham to Malpensa, in the company of a half-dozen businessmen who were chasing a ten o'clock meeting in Milan and a lunch in Venice. A reminder to Veltri of his former life-style.

He was spared the indignity of handcuffs on the plane, though not a reception committee at Malpensa. The businessmen were quite alarmed to see a *carabiniere* car and van pull up alongside them on the apron. No immigration and customs for Veltri. His police escort had him on the *autostrada* within three minutes of landing, using the *carabiniere* van as a road-block behind them to stop the pursuing newsmen. There was no one to see whether they turned east towards the city or west towards the lake.

Two and a half hours later they were climbing into the mountains beyond the lake, winding up a narrow valley road to the isolated village chosen for Veltri's house arrest.

The local *carabiniere* and two of Veltri's men were waiting for them in a deserted piazza by the church.

'Report once a day to the *carabiniere*,' said Assuntino. 'Otherwise, you're free to do what you like.'

Veltri climbed out of the car and looked round at the sparse little village and the mountain peaks above. 'Cheerful place,' he joked to his two waiting bodyguards and nodded at Assuntino as the *magistrato* climbed back into the car.

*

Assuntino stopped his police driver at the lakeside on the way back and offered him lunch. They ordered perch with a bottle of Pinot Grigio on a terrace overlooking the lake, and Assuntino telephoned his long-suffering wife at home in their small Milan flat. Not much hope of seeing her and the kids today. He only had four hours to get down to Genoa and meet Parviz Vaziree with his German off their plane from London.

'Be careful,' his wife implored as always. She'd actually been watching from the window the day the pretty girl on the motorbike had pulled a gun and shot him in the legs on the pavement below their block of flats.

5

Morgan's lunch was a sandwich and a beer and he continued to be hungry. And tired. Laleh, next to him staring at pictures, seemed impervious to hunger or exhaustion. She hadn't even nodded off. Not that Morgan would have noticed if she had.

He'd started off by timing the pictures in an attempt to keep awake. The projectionist was moving them through at an average of three seconds a picture, twenty pictures a minute, twelve hundred an hour. There were ten thousand on file under 'Arabs and Mediterranean', and only seven hours before they had to leave for the train. But then pictures were always a shot in the dark. After an hour or so the faces all begin to look the same.

Elgin's profile appeared like a hand making animals for kids with shadows on the wall. He filled the screen between two pictures and, having made his presence felt, disappeared.

'You know where the buzzer is,' said Morgan to Laleh. 'If you see a face you like the look of just push the button.'

He slid open the door and followed Elgin through the projection cubicle and up the corridor to the 'people's palace' – the Gents in the basement.

'I've been trying to get hold of you for three days.'

Elgin, finger to lips, wedged the door of the toilets shut and walked up the line of basins, turning on the taps.

'I dare say they can even bug bogs if they want to.'

'They?'

'Whoever "they" are.' Morgan was staring at Elgin's ill-fitting and ill-matched clothes. 'I've been to Guatemala,' said Elgin. 'This is my tropical outfit.'

'Why have you taken me off the case?'

'Have I done that?'

'A telex was sent with your name on it.'

'Any damn fool can send a telex.'

Morgan smiled. 'That's what I told Dorff.' Elgin had turned hot as well as cold taps on. The toilet, long and chapel-like, was beginning to fill with steam. 'Guatemala's hardly your patch,' said Morgan.

'No. One of the drugs liaison officers asked me to go out. A principal in a cocaine network said he was ready to talk, but only to me. When I got out there he'd been run over by a tram. They get their bicycle wheels caught in the tramlines. Not that he'd ever ridden a bicycle.'

'I didn't know there were trams in Guatemala.'

Elgin looked puzzled for a moment. 'No. There probably aren't.' He disappeared into one of the WCs and pulled the chain. 'I was told about the telex,' he said as he reappeared. 'There's no way of finding out who sent it. It was in-house of course, but the operator doesn't remember who handed it in.'

'Does that mean I'm back on the case?'

Elgin turned away to survey the steam and the line of urinals. 'We had the television people in here recently. The BBC doing a documentary on the work of Interpol. I stood next to one of them in here. He was pissing pure whiskey. I could smell it.'

'I was asking – '

'I heard what you said, Morgan. It doesn't seem to me you've exactly left the case.'

'Officially, at the moment I'm on leave. If you ask for it, the red file will be on your desk.'

Elgin nodded. 'That would be a precaution. I imagine you've done nothing rational and illegal like make photocopies.' He disappeared into another WC to pull another chain. 'I also assume,' he said, 'your vacation is taking you to Italy.'

Morgan watched him reappear.

'It's on the movement sheet this morning,' said Elgin. 'Mr Veltri's extradition granted. And Mr Vaziree's presence requested for two days to complete the Italian side of the investigation.'

'Like someone moving pieces round the board.'

Elgin nodded. 'Article three of our charter,' he said. 'No politics. It always irritates me when someone in our organization violates that article. It's an insult to one's intelligence.' Elgin looked up at Morgan. 'Do you have any support in Italy?'

'Unofficially. I've asked Reg to meet us at the frontier.'

'Reg?'

'Regina Segantini. Used to be attached to an anti-terrorist squad. She was infiltrating active units in one of the northern universities. Red Brigades and Black Brigades. She's not fond of political lies.'

'Clearly one of your admirers.' Elgin blew his nose. The steam was loosening his sinus. 'And the good-looking lady in the viewing room?'

'Laleh Colraine. The wife of an American diplomat in London. And a close friend of an American journalist who's been investigating Veltri for the last six months. The diplomat is Caleb Colraine; the journalist is Ralph Curtiss – if they could be checked out?'

Elgin nodded.

'It could also be useful to know when Mr Veltri last visited Russia.'

'More difficult but not impossible. Anything else?'

'There's a couple of English people. They have links with Vaziree. An Ashley Buchanan and his daughter.'

Elgin smiled. 'I know Ashley.'

'The old school tie, I suppose.'

'You have an old school yourself, Morgan. Tonbridge, wasn't it?'

'It never seems to work for me.'

Elgin looked at Morgan's scruffy clothes. 'Try wearing the tie.'

Elgin moved towards the door. 'Ashley is ex-Foreign Office. Ex-one or two other things as well, I would imagine. Works for Amnesty International sometimes. His expertise is also sometimes called upon by the oil companies.'

'And the daughter?'

'A red lamb. Very close to Parviz Vaziree at one time, I believe.' Elgin pulled the wedge from under the door. 'Look after Parviz if you can.'

'Elgin, I am not qualified as a bodyguard.'

'Good heavens, no. All you can hope to do is outmanoeuvre them. Intuit. Identify the enemy. Use the honourable and democratic institutions of law and order.'

Elgin opened the door, almost colliding with one of the French heads of group.

'Pardon,' muttered Elgin in his best French.

The man, elderly and elegant, stared at the wedge in Elgin's hand.

'*Le vice Anglais,*' said Elgin with a shrug and a smile, leaving Morgan to turn off the steaming taps under the Frenchman's puzzled and somewhat baleful glare.

6

There had been nothing of Sasan to identify except the clothes he had been wearing at the crematorium. And the photograph in the passport, recognized, apparently, by the man who had clipped his ticket on the station.

Parviz was asked to swear an affidavit to establish Sasan's true identity but, once that formality was completed in the presence of the coroner, the English police seemed only too anxious to get rid of him. He and Dorff were driven with blue flashing light and siren at high speed across south London and down the M23 to Gatwick, where British Caledonian had been persuaded or coerced into delaying departure for them.

'Clean sheets tonight, Garibaldi. Linen sheets.'

Parviz had no idea where in Italy he was being taken. A different set of uniforms met them off the plane, Assuntino with them, and they drove in a two-car convoy over viaducts and through tunnels in a high-speed funnel of heavy trucks and blind corners, the worst of which Parviz began to recognize. They were on their way to Veltri's seaside villa at Portofino: blue sky and hot sun and cocktails on one of the dozen terraces that fell away from the villa to the sea? Parviz imagined that on this occasion it would not be quite like that.

'You're wasting your time,' he told Assuntino, as the cars wound along the narrow corniche and down into the village. They walked from the piazza, where the road ended, along the cobbled alley to the harbour in strange procession – uniformed *carabiniere* and a plain-clothed colleague, the blond Dorff, Assuntino looking like a university don, and Parviz looking, thought Parviz, like a beggar from the kasbah.

But Portofino took not a blind piece of notice, half asleep in the afternoon sun. Beggars and billionaires, they all came daily in their visiting dozens, and the odd policeman escorting a villain or a VIP was nothing out of the ordinary. Perhaps a local shopkeeper or two watched and wondered for a moment when they saw the procession turn up the endless steps onto the promontory beyond the harbour. They'd been reading of Veltri at odd intervals in the newspapers this last ten days and knew *la povera signora* was as usual all alone in the villa.

She was waiting for them, poised and careful at the head of the steps, shaking hands politely with the *magistrato* and looking beyond him with a brief smile for Parviz. 'I'm sure Mr Vaziree will tell you,' she said in clear English, 'there are no secrets to hide in this house.'

7

The early-morning-to-late-afternoon Concorde from New York landed in a cloud of spray. Cal Colraine had followed the briefing in Washington with a breakfast session at the United Nations. His body was well adrift in jet lag when he walked out of the VIP back door at Heathrow to his waiting Cadillac. He saw Ashley Buchanan waiting for him under an umbrella on the sidewalk, his daughter behind him, sheltering in the lee of the building.

'Your embassy phoned,' said Ashley. 'They asked me to meet you here.'

Cal nodded, looking beyond Ashley at Annie. 'Asked *you*.'

'My father doesn't drive,' said Annie. 'And we don't all get Concordes and Cadillacs laid on for our commuting.'

Cal looked back at Ashley. 'Sasan is dead.'

Ashley's hand pinched the top of his nose, frowning deeply. 'Oh my God.' He was genuinely shocked and upset.

Annie was hard and angry. 'Dead, how?' she asked.

'Thrown under a train. Murdered.'

'News travels fast across the Atlantic,' said Annie.

'Our people have their own contacts with British Intelligence.'

'Perhaps they were expecting it to happen.'

Cal turned away to open the rear door of the Cadillac

and touched Ashley on the arm: 'Can we have two words together?'

Ashley folded his umbrella to climb into the back of the car with him.

Cal watched the chauffeur stow his bag on the front seat. 'Wait outside a moment, will you, Sam.'

Annie watched, wet under the rain, as the chauffeur hoisted an umbrella and stood patiently by the car. If he'd been black, she thought, the image would be perfect.

'Washington has authorized me to talk with Shaheen Shaheenee and Parviz Vaziree,' Cal was saying inside the car. 'Is Sasan's death likely to affect anything?'

Ashley was still rubbing his forehead. 'It means that people and time are running out. Shaheenee and Parviz are the only two of any authority left on the outside. And no one inside is in a position to negotiate.'

'But you still maintain they're a credible political force?'

'At the last count there were five-and-a-half-million known supporters inside the country. They can't all have been killed.'

Cal was silent for a moment. 'This is in absolute confidence – we have established contact with a moderate and rather ambitious group within the present regime, on the religious side. They would be looking for a political partnership.'

'Both Parviz and Shaheen are Muslim.'

'Where *is* Parviz?'

'Italy. My sources tell me the judicial enquiry has transferred out there. Mr Veltri withdrew his appeal against extradition. I do have to say I am very concerned for the safety of both Shaheen and Parviz.'

'Where's Shaheen?'

'The indications are he is also in Italy. In hiding.'

'Then I suggest a meeting in Italy. I've asked the State Department that you should participate in the talks –

174

at our expense, naturally. Though I imagine you're representing other interests as well?'

'They are not conflicting interests.'

Again Cal was silent for a moment. 'I believe,' he said, 'your daughter might have conflicting interests.'

'That is possible.'

'Her presence in Italy would not be a good idea.'

Ashley was silent.

Cal held out his hand. 'Washington appreciates your initiative in setting up this situation. Which is why I offer you my complete confidence. I think I share with you a belief that Shaheenee and Vaziree constitute one half of a possible solution.'

Annie watched as the two men shook hands in the back of the car. Then her father climbed out and the chauffeur climbed in.

Ashley shook his head as he watched the limousine move away. 'Either the Americans understand a great deal, or they understand next to nothing at all.' He looked round at Annie. 'There *is* to be a meeting. In Italy.'

'And he's taking you with him?'

Ashley steered Annie back towards their own battered yellow Renault. 'I don't think,' he said carefully, 'it would be a very good idea for you to come.'

'You mean, Daddy, the Americans don't think it would be a very good idea.' She unlocked the car. 'I'll do what I please and what I think is for the best. I certainly shall not abandon Parviz to their hands.'

Ashley looked at her. Annie's hair was wet and her blazing eyes glared at him over the roof of the car. 'We're both seeking the same thing for him and his country,' he said.

'We're both seeking the opposite, you and I,' Annie replied. 'We just happen to be using the same road. Daddy, your solution is not what old Vaziree died for.'

'No more is yours,' Ashley replied coldly.

They sat, silent and wet, in the car until finally father

put hand on daughter's knee. 'I dare say you might be gone by the morning.'

'I dare say.'

'I shall leave messages for you at the consulate in Milan.' Ashley looked down at his hands and round at the floor of the car embarrassed. 'Did I not have an umbrella?'

'I think you've just donated it to the American Embassy.'

8

It was nearly six o'clock when Laleh pressed the buzzer to stop the projection, the fourth or fifth time she'd done so, though on this occasion she had no doubts about the face on the screen in front of her: a handsome face, the younger of the two Arabs she had seen on Twyford Station and at the Soho flat. Morgan took the reference card from records – a number with no name, the picture three years old and taken on a terrorist training camp in Libya: '*Possible member of the PLO, the Habashi group, but nothing known for certain.*'

Morgan asked for the picture and particulars to be wired to McGovern in London, placed a copy of the photograph in the red file and signed the file back to Elgin in his office upstairs.

'What about the second man?' asked Laleh.

'You've been through three and a half thousand faces,' said Morgan looking at his watch. 'And we have a train to catch.' He nodded at the telephone on the table. 'Hadn't you better check up with London?'

Laleh looked at him in surprise.

'You need to know where and when your husband is meeting Parviz.'

Laleh called home and found Cal, already bemused by her message on the kitchen board, now even more perplexed when she told him she was calling from Paris.

But that was all she did tell him, mentioning nothing about the two Arabs, nor the fact of Sasan's death. Cal similarly told her nothing beyond the facts of his intended meeting with Parviz – husband and wife suddenly on tiptoe around each other, aware of their own suspicion and the other's mistrust.

'My husband meets Parviz in Milan on Monday,' Laleh told Morgan as they walked down the hill in St Cloud looking for a taxi.

'You don't seem sure of his part in all of this.'

Laleh shrugged, silent for a moment. 'Someone's pulling the strings,' she said eventually, 'and I'm one of the strings. It's a very uncomfortable feeling when you think it may be someone near to you.'

The rush-hour had absorbed all the taxis and they walked across the bridge to the Métro at Porte de St Cloud. Forty minutes and two changes later they emerged into the echoing bustle of the Gare de Lyons to look for the *Galilei* and the sleeping-car destined for Venice, unaware as they checked into two adjoining berths that the very face Laleh had picked out in the projection room was boarding the same train four coaches down in the second-class couchettes.

Laleh had felt all day as though someone else's motor was pushing her along, holding her eyes open, keeping her mind alert. Now, as she sat down on the bed in her berth, it was as though the someone else had turned that motor off. The momentum of a sleepless night and day had finally run down, the 'high' subsiding into sheer exhaustion. She'd even nodded off on the Métro, relying on Morgan to stay awake and pull them out at Odéon and Châtelet.

At some point last night or today she'd stopped asking herself whether or not she trusted him. Even Roundie dancing had murmured at her, 'He's kind of solid.' Though he'd also murmured, 'Don't fall for him, Lal,' with the inevitable laugh.

She already had fallen for him in a sort of way, perhaps from that very first day before she even knew who he

178

was, looking round and seeing him as he ordered a bottle of wine with his breakfast in the dining-car. She'd subsequently decided he was a man her father would have liked, policeman or not. She would like to show him her father's articles and poems one day. Read them to him in Spanish. Watch his face change, which it did so dramatically when he smiled.

Laleh stood up and looked at her face in the mirror over the tiny basin. The door was ajar behind and she seemed to see it move, as though someone in the corridor had been watching her and then moved away. She looked out, both ways, up and down the corridor. Morgan's door was shut; a rather beautiful red-haired girl was struggling with luggage three doors beyond. Laleh dismissed her sudden feeling of unease and went back inside her compartment to open her bag.

What she hadn't seen was the Arab face hiding in the vacant berth beyond Morgan's, to re-emerge as she closed her door: neatly built, with a trim moustache, and eyes that blazed at the red-haired girl with such intensity the girl felt suddenly and wholly vulnerable, as though he'd stripped her naked there in the corridor.

The killer zigzagged away down three crowded corridors beyond the sleeping-car, whistles blowing on the platform outside. His companion had bribed the couchette conductor to find them vacant bunks – in a carriage that seemed populated entirely with nuns and novices. How they had fluttered and flustered when the two dark Arabs walked in. And how they fluttered now, holding up a blanket to undress behind as the killer lay back on his bunk and closed his eyes.

The train was already moving at speed when Laleh returned to the carpeted corridor and exchanged smiles with an old lady standing by a window two doors down. The old lady was watching the last lights of Paris fade away, as though she felt she'd never see the city again. A Parisienne departing or an Italian returning home, Laleh wondered.

179

The old lady turned back to her compartment door with another smile and a nod for Laleh.

'*Bonsoir, madame,*' said Laleh.

'*Bonne nuit.*' The old lady closed her door and the corridor was empty again.

Laleh turned to knock at Morgan's door. The door, unlatched, swung open. His bag was on the bed but the compartment was empty. Again, Laleh felt a sudden sense of unease. A fear.

The sleeping-car attendant appeared at the end of the corridor, his arms full of bedding, then disappeared again into one of the berths. Laleh heard or sensed something behind her and spun round. Morgan was standing there grinning, a tray of food in either hand, a bottle of wine in either pocket.

Laleh laughed. 'I thought for a moment you'd abandoned me.'

Morgan handed her one of the trays.

'I wouldn't even have known there was food on the train. Is that why they call you Railway Joe?'

Morgan nodded at the open door of his berth. 'Were you going to steal my bag?'

'The door was open.'

'Perhaps someone else contemplated stealing it.'

Morgan moved the bag and they sat side by side on the bed, trays on their knees. Morgan picked up a morsel of salad, looked at it and shook his head. 'Plastic food in France. Trains ain't what they used to be.'

Laleh smiled: 'When was Railway Joe?'

'When the railways started running again after the war.' Morgan poured and drank a plastic beaker of wine. 'Railway Joe was very young and used to wait for the trains on dark platforms in the middle of the night and climb on board with his torch.'

They ate for a moment in silence, both of them remembering nightmares from long ago.

'We always seemed to cross frontiers by night,' she said eventually. 'Uniforms banging the door and switch-

180

ing on the light or shining torches in our faces. "*Passaporto. Dokumente, bitte. Passeport.*"' She laughed. 'My poor mother never had the right piece of paper and we'd usually end up being turned off the train with our one suitcase onto some dark platform in the middle of the night.' She looked round at him.

Morgan nodded. 'Yes – that was sometimes me. The keen young face in the demob suit standing in front of the uniforms holding the torch. Italy, France, Germany, Austria and all the frontiers to the east. That was my territory. Railway Joe, recruited from Military Intelligence for the control of migration and smuggling. Spot checks in the middle of the night to catch displaced persons in displaced Europe.' Morgan poured and drank another beaker of wine. 'Railway Joe wasn't a very nice person.'

They'd both finished their trays of pre-packed food. 'Is that where you met McGovern?'

'There were a lot of Italian immigrants in those days,' Morgan replied. 'Coming over by train, into Dover and Folkestone, and treated like cattle. McGovern used to sniff out the smugglers. Sit on the boat-train with them when they thought they'd got through. There'd always be someone boasting about the extra bottles of wine they'd brought in. He'd turn them round at Victoria and take them back to the boat. Then he had the bright idea of me in London. Italian cop against Italian Soho. We had to work together. Until I cracked up.' Morgan laughed and drank again. 'Conflict of loyalties. Six months' leave with a nervous breakdown and back to Interpol. McGovern was disgusted. He has a great contempt for weakness.'

'I don't,' said Laleh.

Morgan looked at her; looked away; then stood up and gathered their two trays. 'I'll bring you coffee,' he said.

What an unusual and complete confession, he thought, embarrassed as he turned away up the corridor. Even

Rudi, who'd fought that Soho battle with him, had never known the full story about Railway Joe.

The killer saw him go, watching through the glass of the connecting door at the far end of the sleeping-car. As soon as Morgan was out of sight the Arab moved through the connecting door into the carpeted corridor of the sleeping-car, where the sounds of the train were more subdued. He presumably remembered the numbers 27/28 on the woman's door, but as he approached, so the uniformed attendant reappeared to sit at his desk at the far end of the car. The Arab turned back the way he'd come.

By the time Morgan had queued in the self-service buffet and twice walked the length of half the train, Laleh had returned to her compartment. Morgan knocked and called through the door: 'Coffee?'

'I thought it was someone knocking to see my papers,' she said with a laugh when she opened the door. She was in her dressing-gown, her face already cleaned of its make-up. 'I'm sorry,' she said, a hand to her cheek. 'I was falling asleep.'

'That's how you always should be seen,' said Morgan. 'No mask and no painted smile.'

'Do I have a painted smile?'

'Sometimes.' Morgan handed her a covered plastic beaker of coffee and held up two miniatures of calvados. 'Nightcap in your toothmug?'

Laleh emptied one of the little bottles into the glass in its metal stand over her basin. She turned to raise it at Morgan. 'And when do you lose your mask?'

Morgan twisted the cap off his bottle and sipped at it. 'I have no mask.'

'You distance yourself,' said Laleh. 'Like you're standing there now.'

182

'Waiting for your passport? Your two passports.'

'I don't know what you're waiting for if you don't tell me.'

'I'm not very good at saying the things I'd like to say.' Morgan looked away. 'There never seems any justification for someone like me to say them at all.' He looked back at her and smiled. 'We shall know each other for seven days.'

'Ships passing.'

'Strangers passing. Shadows passing.'

Laleh reached out a hand and touched his face. 'Am I a shadow?'

Morgan took her hand and kissed it. 'No.'

'As you are not a stranger to me. Two displaced persons in displaced Europe?'

'Except that you have found a refuge.'

'As you will when you are ready.'

Morgan shook his head. 'I think somehow I have trapped myself in a no-man's-land.'

He released her hand and stepped back into the corridor.

'If I knock on the wall, will you be there?' she asked.

'Fast asleep, I imagine,' he replied with a smile and closed the door.

But he lay down on his bed wideawake instead and fully dressed, staring at the blue lamp in the ceiling.

9

Laleh and the old lady must have moved at the same time, both in dressing-gowns, both bound for the toilet at the end of the sleeping-car. Laleh was the first to appear in the corridor, clearly seen by the killer from the far side of the connecting door. The killer and his colleague slipped through the door, out of sight inside the toilet. They didn't see the second of the compartments open and the old lady shuffle out ahead of Laleh. Laleh turned with a patient smile back to her own compartment to wait. She would later remember hearing a sudden faint roar as though a door had been opened at the end of the car.

It happened so fast the old lady was hardly aware of anything – just the first shock of the dark figure in front of her when she opened the toilet. His hand gagged her, his other arm turned her and as the second Arab opened the external door, tipped her into the rushing black void outside, both men in that instant, and too late, realizing their mistake.

Laleh, rubbing cream into her face and neck, waited another five minutes before walking again to the toilet. The corridor was cold, the partition door before the toilet swinging. As Laleh stepped through, the blast of wind hit her and she found herself staring at that rushing black void through the open door. If the Arabs had waited for her, one little push would have been enough. Instead she backed away and turned, running up the corridor to bang at Morgan's door.

184

'I think someone's fallen off the train,' she said, breathless and very frightened when he opened his door. It was as though she knew instinctively what had happened. 'An old lady. She came out of her compartment ahead of me,' she said, still breathless, following Morgan down the corridor. 'We were both going to the toilet. I returned to my own compartment to wait. When I went back the outside door was wide open.'

Morgan pushed the outside door shut against the blast of wind. 'Which compartment did she come out of?' he asked Laleh, his two hands on her shoulders to try and calm her. He also had guessed the sequence of events.

The old lady's compartment was empty, a cigarette in the ashtray burnt down its full length, a book lying on the pillow.

Morgan walked Laleh back to her own compartment. 'Lock yourself in,' he told her, 'and don't open the door to anyone.'

Morgan looked at his watch. Another quarter of an hour or so to Vallorbe. The French police would hold them all for ever if he told anyone on this side of the frontier. So would the Swiss, come to that. Best sit tight and wait a while, not forgetting the unfortunate old lady might still be alive.

The platform at Vallorbe was cold, the frontier police, both French and Swiss, stamping their feet to keep warm. Morgan stepped off the train, using his ID card to pass the police check. He found a pay-phone downstairs in the station hall and, as an anonymous caller, rang the police at Frasne, twenty minutes back up the line. He told them of a body by the track on the Andelot side of Frasne, about five minutes from the station.

Morgan returned to the train and, once they were moving again and inside Switzerland, he dug out the sleeping-car attendant, finding him in the end berth with a bottle of wine. '*Oh merde!*' he said when Morgan showed him his ID card and told him one of his passengers had fallen off the train.

The two of them examined the old lady's berth. 'Maybe she sleep with someone else,' the attendant suggested, well used to bed-hopping up and down his corridors.

Morgan showed him the old lady's passport picture. 'She's seventy years old,' he said. 'Even for a French girl that's pushing it a bit.'

The attendant sat gloomily on the old lady's bed, visions of his free day in Venice already receding. Morgan tapped his watch. 'The Swiss police would hold us all night if we stop the train here. I suggest we wait a couple of hours and you officially discover her disappearance at Domodossola.'

The attendant nodded reluctantly.

'In the meantime,' Morgan went on, 'I want to see every passport on this train.'

'*Pourquoi?*'

'The old lady didn't fall. And the two men who pushed her didn't get off at Vallorbe.'

The sleeping-car attendant walked with him carriage to carriage through the train, asking each of his colleagues for their piles of passports and tickets, Morgan scrutinizing every photograph. They interrupted their search briefly for the three-minute stop at Lausanne, the attendant on one side of the train, Morgan on the other, to check that no one got off.

Not long afterwards, Morgan found what he was looking for in one of the second-class couchettes – the face of the Arab identified by Laleh in Paris, inside a passport issued from an embassy in Tripoli.

The couchette conductor looked at the face and remembered clearly the two men who had bribed their way into a compartment full of nuns and novices. '*Ils étaient deux* – ' he said, and picked out the second passport. Morgan looked at the killer's face for the first time – the moustache, the eyes, the name, the description.

He thanked conductor and attendant, borrowed a pass-key, and walked quietly up the corridor to identify the compartment – and lock the door. Anyone wanting the toilet would now have to bang and shout for the conductor. And the conductor had agreed not to open the door without first referring to Morgan.

Morgan walked on towards the front of the train. A young novice and an older nun were deep in conversation at the end of the couchette car, the older woman waving smoke away with one hand and guiltily hiding her cigarette as Morgan passed. Morgan wondered how many of them had been naughty together in the toilet tonight.

10

Parviz, Veltri, Annie – even Rudi in Soho: they were all wideawake at half past two that Sunday morning. Rudi was mopping with cloth and bucket where the rain was leaking through the boarded-up skylight; Annie was in the Oxford bed where she'd lain with Parviz on Tuesday night, listening now to the rain on the slates and wondering if the 8.50 to Paddington would leave her enough time to cross London for the boat-train.

Parviz could hear the sea from the guest-room in the villa. His eyes were open, watching moonlight through the shutters. He was thinking of the simple kindness of his hostess, Signora Veltri, who had insisted on taking him down into the village to eat dinner on a restaurant terrace above the harbour, while Dorff and the Italian plain-clothes man were forced to watch from the outside once they'd studied the prices on the menu. Wild mushrooms, Parviz had eaten.

High in the mountains, the church clock rang on the half hour, day and night, ten yards away through the wall. At each thirty-minute interval Veltri had been waking until his brain was throbbing with a half-hour pulse. He too had thought tonight of moonlight on a sea still warm from the summer; and a fifty-dollar dinner at the Pitosforo down by the harbour, with a plate of the *Boletus edulis* he had searched for unsuccessfully in the woods above the village. It was cold tonight in the mountains.

Not far to the north and six thousand feet below ground, the train crossed the watershed between the Rhône and the Po. Ten minutes later it poured out of the twelve-mile tunnel and began the winding descent down the valley and into Italy.

Morgan was standing at the front of the train, watching the locomotive through the glass of the connecting doors – OIOIOI the engine number, red and still Swiss, until the frontier change-over at Domodossola. He saw the pantograph tear flame from the overhead power-line, a brief illumination like a photographer's white flash over wet stone walls and pine trees.

He hoped that Reg was waiting for him.

11

It was nearly two years since Reg had last seen Morgan – slipping one late night from her bed and dressing quietly not to wake her, for he had already said goodbye. Insofar as he ever did. He'd told her that very day she was the only woman who had ever accepted his aloneness and left it alone. Not, she supposed, that he ever gave anyone an alternative.

Besides which, Regina had lived for long enough alone herself, in mind if not in body, to know how untouchable aloneness becomes.

She watched the train threading its way through the intersection before the station. The half-dozen frontier police with her on the platform were waiting like statues – asleep on their feet.

Morgan was standing down on the steps of a sleeping car by an open door, holding his hand out for her as the train slid past. She'd thought she was meeting him, not joining him, but took his hand and swung on board. He showed her the photographs of the two Arabs in their passports as the train eased to a halt.

'They've killed three times already. They're one above the other in couchettes, top bunk and middle bunk to the right.' He grinned at her. 'Thanks for coming, Reg.'

'I thought I was taxi-driving tonight.'

'You can taxi-drive later. When we go in through that door, we have to make them believe we have guns in our hands.'

'Do *they* have guns?'

190

'I don't suppose we'll have time to ask them.'

Reg shook her head, not pleased, and they positioned themselves in silence, one each side of the door, Morgan with the passkey in his hand. He prayed the lock would turn with ease. Reg nodded at him. He turned the key and she pulled the door open.

'On your feet!' he yelled as he charged in, hands grabbing for the upper bunk. 'On your feet! Hands out in front of you!'

'*Nessuno si muove!*' Reg was shouting behind him, her hands grabbing at the middle bunk.

Nuns or novices woke up screaming.

Morgan dragged his man off the upper bunk, rolling him off, a knee into his groin, as he tried to struggle, spinning him face to the bunks and kicking his legs out from under him.

Reg's bunk was empty and she turned to help Morgan, frisking the Arab, bringing a fist up hard between his legs as he tried to move again.

Morgan was shouting.

He banged back into the corridor, walking up the car pulling open the other doors and turning on the lights. The toilet door at the end was locked and he kicked and banged at it, until a hand behind restrained him – one of the policemen from the platform, the couchette conductor and the sleeping-car attendant with him.

'*Si calmi*,' said the policeman. '*Stia calmo. Adesso facciamo noi.*'

It took them twenty minutes to search the train with guards on both sides and at either end. To no avail. The second Arab, the killer, had vanished.

Morgan opened Laleh's door with his borrowed passkey. She was asleep. He perched on the bed beside her and touched her cheek, stroking it until she opened her eyes and looked at him. 'Did you find the old lady?' she asked.

191

Morgan shook his head.

'What happened?'

'Your two Arabs were travelling with us. It was meant to be you they threw off the train.'

Laleh stared at him.

'We found one of them.'

'And the other?'

'Vanished.' Morgan showed her the killer's passport. 'Wherever he is, he's going to be in trouble without this.' Morgan stroked hair back from her face.

'Where are we?'

'Domodossola.'

She sat up in alarm. 'We have to get off.'

'They'll be taking statements up and down the train for the next hour or so. I'll come for you in good time.'

'I'll start getting ready.'

Morgan stood up. 'I'm afraid you haven't had much sleep.'

'What should I tell them? The police, I mean.'

'What happened. Without mentioning the Arabs.'

'Has anything been done about the old lady?'

The French police confirmed the old lady's death half an hour later. Her body had been found, back broken, across the concrete lip of a drain culvert at the side of the track three kilometres on the Paris side of Frasne.

12

There was already light in the sky behind the mountains before the police were ready to release the train. Reg and Laleh met in the door of a by now sleepless sleeping-car.

'*Piacere*,' Laleh said with a smile, in her best Italian.

'How do you do,' came Reg's reply, without a smile.

Down in the subway the younger Arab, held hand-cuffed against the wall, stared at Laleh as she passed.

'How did they know we were on this train?' she asked Morgan.

'They were either waiting for us when we arrived yesterday morning and followed us; or someone in Paris told them. Our berths were booked through the office.'

'Your Mr Elgin?'

'I hope to God not.'

Reg's car was waiting in the deserted piazza outside, the streets still sleeping and empty as she drove them round the back of the town and up into the hills.

Laleh was asleep again on the back seat, her head on Morgan's shoulder.

'Have you called me out in the middle of the night to be chauffeur on your honeymoon, Joe?'

'She's tired, Reg. That's all.' Morgan smiled at Reg in the mirror. 'You remember what it's like to be tired.'

'For weeks on end. Tired of being frightened.'

Morgan looked down at Laleh. Her eyes were open. 'Reg would have medals,' he said, 'if anyone could tell the world what she'd done.'

Reg laughed. 'If anyone had told the world what I'd done, Joe, I was dead five years ago.'

The car seemed to climb into the dawn and leave the night in the valley below. By the time they'd circled the hairpins up into the last village, the grey light of early morning was complete, though nothing yet moved among the houses. Reg parked in the piazza. Morgan disengaged from the sleeping Laleh to swing himself out of the car and into the cold clear air. He heard the car door open and shut again behind him. Laleh moved to his shoulder as he walked to the edge of the piazza by the church and looked over the valley.

'My father was born twenty miles away in one of the other valleys,' he said after a while. 'We used to come back every summer until the war started. Then it was six years before he came home. As soon as the trains started running again he did come back. Rudi and I were with him. When my father saw these mountains from the train a hundred miles away, he started to cry. I can remember him doing it.'

Laleh took his arm. Morgan looked round at the car. Reg was fast asleep, Behind them the church clock gathered itself for a strike.

'Let's pull these people out of bed,' said Morgan.

First the village *carabiniere*; then Veltri's two body-guards; finally Mr Veltri himself, wrapped up in a woollen jacket and wearing a cap against the cold. They sat at a stone table outside the village bar, the *carabiniere* hovering behind them, the bodyguards at an adjoining table. The bar itself was not yet open.

'I think we speak in English,' said Veltri, with a smile for the *carabiniere*. He turned to Morgan. 'I thought they send you away.'

'They did. My presence here is entirely unofficial.'

'To ask me questions? Or to give me news?'

'Sasan is dead,' said Morgan.

Veltri stared at him. It was difficult to tell whether his look expressed surprise, disappointment or apprehension.

'You are running out of people and out of time,' suggested Morgan, still watching him carefully.

'How you mean "running out"?'

'You invested an enormous amount of money building an oil refinery and leasing oil-tankers eight years ago when you believed old Vaziree and Shaheenee would come to power. Unfortunately, they then lost control of the revolution you, among many others, helped to foster. It is not illogical to assume you have since talked with the Russians in the hope they might help Shaheenee and his party.'

Veltri was watching him, poker-faced and silent.

'They come to power and your price is the oil concession,' suggested Morgan. He was guessing wildly.

'What do you want from me?' asked Veltri.

'We need to find Shaheenee,' said Laleh.

Veltri looked at her without reply.

'Parviz Vaziree arrived in Italy yesterday,' said Morgan. 'We expect Shaheenee to try and make contact with him – and when he does, like the others, to meet with an accident.'

'If we knew where he was hiding,' said Laleh, 'it would be easier to protect him.'

'Why do you think *I* hide Shaheenee?'

'Sasan arrived in England with Italian passport, Italian driving licence, Italian ID card, the whole lot. I don't believe he could have organized that by himself. Sasan was also Shaheenee's most trusted colleague. Where he was hiding, Shaheenee would also be hiding.'

Veltri laughed. 'Damn good business your mind does not work for the CIA.'

'Why CIA?' asked Laleh.

'Because they are probably CIA killings, lady.'

Laleh looked incredulous. 'They can't be. Last night they tried to kill me.'

'So now you have real credentials!'

'They're Arabs, these killers.'

'The Arabs are hired men. The CIA or KGB hired them. Maybe the British. But the British no longer kill – except in Ireland.' Veltri took a notepad from his pocket, and wrote down an address on one side, a message on the other. 'Shaheenee hides himself without my help. This is the only point of contact.' Veltri tore off the piece of paper and handed it to Laleh. 'He is an old and very frightened man.'

Morgan stood up, cold from the stone bench, pulling up his collar.

Veltri shrugged at the shuttered bar. 'We wait a long time for our coffee in the mornings.' He walked with them to the steps that led back down the hill to the piazza.

'Why did you suddenly decide not to contest extradition and come back here?'

'Love of my country?'

Morgan laughed and led the way down the steps.

Reg, in the car, was still fast asleep, with her head on her arms against the steering-wheel. She woke with a start as Morgan opened the door for Laleh. Veltri stood watching them, his bodyguards behind him. 'I have to say,' he said, 'I believe Parviz and Shaheenee are already dead men. Which means I will be bankrupt.'

'Better to be bankrupt than to be dead,' said Laleh.

The sun had already risen on the higher peaks across the valley as the car circled down the hairpins to leave the village behind, Veltri watching them from the piazza.

'How did you know about the Russians?' Laleh asked Morgan.

'I didn't. I guessed.'

'And the CIA? How does he know?'

'He doesn't. He's also guessing. And wondering if he isn't himself the next target.' Morgan looked out of the window up at the village, isolated on its shoulder of hillside. 'He needs his bodyguards in a place like this.'

13

Parviz woke to reflections of sun on sea dancing through
the shutters and across the wall. He pushed shutter and
window open to feel the warmth of the sun and saw
Signora Veltri sitting at the far side of the terrace in an
angle of the wall where the hillside below fell steeply
down towards the harbour. Parviz could, for a moment,
make believe he was a free man, and tried to imagine
how that might feel again after so long. But he knew as
soon as he opened the door onto the landing, he would
find Dorff waiting for him outside.

The *magistrato* had arrived from his hotel in the village
to sift again through papers in the rooms downstairs.
No part of the villa had been excluded from his search,
but he had as yet found nothing. He looked out of the
window as Parviz crossed the gravel outside to join
Signora Veltri in the corner of the terrace, the maid
following him with a tray of coffee and brioches. Assuntino looked out of the far window across the bay and
down the coast south to Levanto and the Cinque Terre.
Veltri's summer residence was, he guessed, one of the
most expensive villas on the Riviera. Yet no one seemed
to know where his wealth came from – apart from that
quite modest 'Exocet' account in London, a mere five
figures in dollars. His oil interests – a leased oil refinery
and sub-leased oil-tankers – were losing him ten thousand dollars a week. From somewhere a bank was propping him up.

Assuntino turned back to a box of photograph albums

he'd found in one of the upstairs rooms the previous afternoon, one of the volumes faithfully recording, among other 'family' occasions, the original visit of Parviz and his colleagues to this very villa. The *magistrato* had recognized some of the same faces in another, more recent album. So recent, in fact, it hadn't yet been labelled and dated. He picked up the second volume and carried it out onto the terrace, joining Signora Veltri and Parviz at their table.

Signora Veltri watched him sit down. She was careful and guarded as ever.

'Can you tell me who these people are?' asked Assuntino, opening the book at the appropriate page and passing it over.

Signora Veltri looked at the photographs. 'They are friends of my husband,' she said. 'He has many friends.' She handed the book back. 'And girl-friends.'

'Are they Italian friends?'

'No.'

Parviz, as Assuntino intended, had seen and recognized the faces. He gestured at the album. 'May I?'

Assuntino passed the album to him. 'You know them?'

Two faces Parviz was staring at: Farshid and Sasan. 'I *knew* them. They are both recently dead. I think you were aware of their deaths. In England.'

The *magistrato* turned the page onto a photograph of Shaheenee. 'And this man?'

'Shaheen Shaheenee. My father's friend. And most trusted colleague.' There was already a coolness in Parviz's voice. He could see the pictures were recent.

The *magistrato* looked back at Signora Veltri. 'When were these pictures taken?'

Signora Veltri shrugged. 'My husband always takes pictures.'

'This year?'

She shrugged again. 'Maybe.'

Another page turned and Parviz found himself staring

at a picture of Annie. Here at the villa. And, standing with her, a man Parviz had never seen before.

Assuntino was watching him. 'You know the girl?'

Parviz nodded.

'And the man.'

'I imagine he is Italian.'

Again Assuntino passed the book across the table to the Signora. 'Is he Italian?' he asked.

Signora Veltri was silent.

'Do you know this man?'

Still no reply.

'Signora, devo insistere.'

Signora Veltri glanced at Parviz and looked away. 'He was from the Russian Embassy in Rome.'

Parviz closed his eyes: Annie, Farshid, Sasan and Shaheenee with Veltri and the Russians. And neither Annie nor Sasan had said a word of it to him. Parviz stood up and turned away, looking over the wall at the sea two hundred feet below.

The *magistrato* seemed almost as upset as Parviz was. Certainly as angry. He snapped the book shut, laid it on the table and stood up facing Parviz at the wall. 'I think, Mr Vaziree, you have no evidence for me against Signor Veltri. I believe you never did have. I think you and I, we are – *pupazzi* –'

'Puppets,' said the Signora, translating.

'Yes – puppets. Puppets in another game.' Assuntino looked round at Dorff on the far side of the terrace. 'I must tell him you are now free to go back to where you came from.'

Parviz replied in a low voice that even the Signora strained to hear. 'I am a political prisoner. I am asking for asylum.'

The *magistrato* was genuinely reluctant. 'We are informed you are to attend a meeting in Milan with American friends of yours. Your permission will be extended to Tuesday morning. Then you return home.' Assuntino took off his spectacles. 'I'm sorry. We had to promise you would be returned. The promise was made at the highest level.' He turned away, glancing at Signora Veltri. *'Mi dispiace, Signora. Anche per me.'*

14

Sunday on the lakes had held them up; even Reg's pugnacious driving was slowed by the queues of week-end cars, until they stopped at the lakeside trattoria where Assuntino had eaten with his police driver the day before. While waiting for their food on that same terrace, Morgan briefed Reg with the photocopied pages from the file – pages which Laleh herself had also never seen. It was not yet midday and the restaurant was still empty. In the hazy light of an Indian summer across the lake, the talk of death seemed a blasphemy.

'We have to assume,' said Morgan, 'that the killer or his replacement has the support to work as efficiently in Italy as he did in England. On Monday Parviz meets American diplomats. Laleh believes we should find Shaheenee and persuade him to join that meeting and thus give full responsibility to the Americans for their safety.'

Like Assuntino and his police driver, they ate perch and drank Pinot Grigio, and as the restaurant began to fill with Sunday families, returned to the car and the now less crowded lakeside road. By the time they reached the *autostrada*, the city-bound carriageway was empty, and Morgan and Laleh were fast asleep on the back seat.

Reg woke them on the outskirts of Milan, Morgan from the depths of a slow-motion chase with Rudi and McGovern up the corridors of an endless train, Laleh from oblivion.

Morgan looked at Reg in the driving mirror. 'Would

it cause surprise if you went into work on a Sunday?' he asked her.

'Nothing I do surprises anyone any more.'

Morgan looked round at Laleh. 'Regina works at the university. It's quiet and anonymous – and I dare say she has a telephone you can use. Call the embassy in Rome. Find out what arrangements have been made for tomorrow's meeting – but don't tell them where you are. Don't tell anyone where you are.'

They drove through empty streets into the middle of the city. Reg dropped Morgan in the piazza by the castle, and Laleh turned to watch him through the rear window as he crossed the road by the subway, reappeared on the centre island and climbed on board a tram.

She faced front again and caught Reg's eye in the mirror watching her. 'He'll be all right,' she said. Laleh nodded, feeling a little foolish. 'You know Milan?' asked Reg.

'I knew Milan when I was a child,' Laleh replied.

Reg looked at her watch. 'Empty at two o'clock Sunday afternoon, packed out by five. The poor come in on Sunday afternoons to look at the shop-windows while the rich are out in the country or up in the mountains or down by the sea.' She laughed. 'Except today we are told no one is poor.'

Laleh was still watching her in the mirror, wondering if she and Morgan had been lovers. There was certainly a warmth and an understanding between them that Laleh would have to admit she envied. But maybe that closeness had come merely from sharing danger. And, in any case, she thought to herself, it was none of her business.

Laleh glimpsed the cathedral as they passed one corner of the piazza. 'The wedding cake,' Reg said. 'The one moment in history the impeccable good taste of the Milanese deserted them.'

Laleh laughed. 'You are not from Milan?'

'You should hear it in my voice.' Reg changed down a gear in her voice. '*Puro Romano sono!*' She turned the car across a red light the wrong way down a one-way street to park in a long-grassed piazza.

The university was cloistered and cool. Reg nodded to the porter as she led Laleh in through the gate and down one side of the large central courtyard.

'Do you teach here?' asked Laleh.

'I'm just a secretary,' said Reg. 'Administration.'

'Was it here you were working with Morgan?'

'That was another university.'

'Was it very dangerous?'

Reg shrugged. 'It was unpleasant – to win people's trust and friendship, and then betray them.'

'But it was necessary.'

Reg shrugged again. 'Who knows?'

'To get rid of the terrorists?'

'Whoever they are.' She turned with half a smile for Laleh as they skirted the smaller cloister beyond the courtyard. 'In this country there will always be terrorists under one name or another.' Reg unlocked the door of her office upstairs and directed Laleh to the telephone on the desk. 'I'll try to find some coffee.'

The address Veltri had scribbled with the note on the piece of paper was a block of old municipal flats on the south side of the city between the two canals. Façades of balcony and kaleidoscope washing-lines, courtyards and outside stairs – and everywhere a feeling of Sunday torpor. Number 57 on the fifth floor was answered by a tiny sparrow of a man in shirt sleeves, the sound of football coming from his radio inside the house while he scrutinized both Morgan and the piece of paper Veltri had written out.

'It's the first allotment down the other side of the canal,' he said finally. 'About half a mile out beyond the bridges.'

Morgan returned to the canal, crossing by the hump bridge below the church. He watched a coxless four

203

turning across the water by a club boat-house; a couple of taxis being washed on the bank in the shade of the bridge where the ring road passed; an old man sculling, slow and sedate, against the current.

The allotment was hidden behind a creeper-covered fence, its high padlocked gate half-concealed in the foliage, an old woman visible inside hoeing a row of beans, a train shunting on the railway sidings beyond.

'Signora?'

He showed Veltri's note again when she'd shuffled to the gate, and reluctantly she let him in, returning to her hoe without a word. It seemed he was expected to wait, though when he tapped his watch and asked her how long, she shrugged, again without a reply.

Morgan sat on an upturned oil drum listening to the goods train shunting in the yard, swatting at the cloud of flies that had followed him in from the canal, and wishing there'd been a patch of grass to lie down and sleep on.

15

'You've known Morgan a long time,' said Laleh.

Reg shrugged, blowing cigarette smoke through the window and out across the cloister. She had a way of shrugging that didn't seem to move either her head or shoulders. 'Joe comes and goes without much warning. Two years ago I last saw him. Sometimes I think I do not know him at all.' She stubbed out her cigarette and turned to the door. 'Maybe you telephone again.' It was the second time Reg had politely left the room while Laleh was using the phone. If on this occasion she had stayed in the room with her, an encouragement to caution, events might have turned out very differently.

'Mrs Colraine,' said the embassy voice, 'the plane is delayed and your husband has still not yet arrived in Milan. If you tell me where you are, I'll have him call you just as soon as we make contact.'

'All I need to know,' said Laleh, 'are the arrangements he has made for meeting – ' she checked herself successfully.

'Yes?' prompted the embassy voice.

'For meeting someone he's coming over here to meet,' said Laleh lamely. 'I'm meant to be joining them.'

'I'm sorry, Mrs Colraine. I'm only the duty officer. I know nothing about that. If you leave your number, I'll have someone call you.'

Laleh was silent for a moment. 'I'll call again myself later,' she said.

'Mrs Colraine, I've given you his address in Milan. If you'll let me have a contact number, I can arrange for your husband to call you from the airport.'

And this time Laleh succumbed. 'All right,' she said, and read the number off the phone in front of her. 'Milan 540294.'

Morgan had no idea how long the girl had been there watching him. An end-of-afternoon mist was already rising over the bank from the canal; the old woman was pushing her wheelbarrow of weeds to some far corner of the allotment beyond a jungle of full-grown maize. Morgan turned his back on her and faced the shed, unzipping his trousers to pee into a line of beans. He glanced up at the shed when he'd finished and thought for a moment he was looking at a painting – the face of a young Madonna, perhaps a print on cardboard used to patch up the door of the shed. But the Madonna was watching him zip up his trousers and seemed almost to smile. 'I am Firuze,' she said as she pushed open the door. 'You have a message from Sasan Sasanee?'

Her almost-smile was brief; her face returned to grave composure. She was sixteen, maybe seventeen, years old, very slight, rather frail and exquisitely beautiful. She knew immediately by his silence and the look on his face that there was no message from Sasan and guessed soon enough what had happened, though her composure never seemed to waver. At least, not in front of him. She looked at the note Veltri had written, listened to what Morgan had to say, examined his ID card, and watched him with dark and grave brown eyes. When she decided to accept what he said, her instructions to him were brief and precise.

Morgan wondered if she was watching him as he walked away back up the canal bank; wondered how many people she could call on for help; wondered which, if any, of the exiles had been in love with her. Unless, of course, she was Shaheenee's daughter. He heard the rumble of a tram behind him on the far side of the canal and quickened his pace to cross the iron stairs of the old lift bridge that carried a railway siding over the canal and into one of the factories. As he rode the tram back into the centre of the city, the ring roads were beginning to jam with cars and waving scarves as the football crowds left San Siro two miles away. Morgan was in no hurry. The girl had given him three hours and he needed time to think.

Parviz needed time – period. Time to find a way to keep alive.

Signora Veltri's licence for kindness was running out. The *magistrato* had left in the late morning, but she had insisted on keeping Parviz there for lunch and even succeeded in distancing him from Dorff and the Italian plain–clothes man. Parviz imagined that her kindness and intrigue were motivated by her husband's interests, but he was grateful none the less – if appalled at his own helplessness. Even when she'd manoeuvred him into a room alone with a telephone, he had no idea whom he could call. He had no direction in which to turn; and she had no idea how her husband might have tried to help. Annie had given him the number in Oxford. It was the only number he could think to dial – but there was no reply.

At five that afternoon, Dorff marched him down the hill through the Sunday crowds around the harbour, back to the car. They had accommodation booked that night in a hotel complex on the outskirts of Milan.

At the same time, Ashley was sitting in the departure lounge of Terminal Two at Heathrow. He had taken the bus in from Oxford. When the Alitalia flight was called he found himself seated with Cal Colraine and Blind

Hugh, booked into the same front row by the American Embassy in London.

Annie was more slumped than sitting, staring through two windows across the corridor at gloomy northern France as the train threaded its way into Lille. An Italian family was in occupation of the entire compartment except for her seat by the door, salame and peeled orange scenting the air while they worked a steady way through the food in their plastic bags. Annie had budgeted for a roll and a beer on the train – but there was of course no catering. Sooner or later she'd have to accept the Italians' offer to share their picnic.

16

Morgan noticed the car as he walked down the long façade of the university. Most of the piazza was empty; Reg's brown Alfa was parked at the far end, a few bicycles were locked into their wheel-grips. The white Mercedes pulled up on the pavement outside the shuttered bar opposite the university entrance. Morgan wasn't sure why he glanced at it a second time – until he registered the Swiss number-plate, Geneva, and the glass so dark the interior of the car could not be clearly seen. He had an impression there were two people inside.

The precaution of noticing and memorizing its registration number was entirely automatic. Habit in a situation already menacing. The second precaution was to ask Reg to take them out of a back entrance – an hour later and in the darkness. Though his paranoia did acknowledge that someone efficient would have covered all the entrances and exits. Besides which, Reg herself had to double back round the building to pick up her own car.

It was a pity paranoia didn't also suggest calling the whole thing off.

Reg was 'back-up', parked on an empty taxi-rank at Porta Ticinese by the taxi call-phone.

Morgan and Laleh had ridden out in a cab down along the canal a mile or so short of the church and the allotments beyond.

'*Ci vuole un temporale*,' said the bald taxi-driver and fanned a hand in front of his face. The air was getting heavy, he meant. Tomorrow will be too hot, he went on. Then maybe tomorrow night, bang-bang. Thunderstorm. And the autumn begins.

He swung the taxi off the canal road to pull up in front of an *osteria*. Morgan paid him off, tipping him, he told him, for his pretty face and the weather forecast.

The *osteria* was rough and ready, and noisy for a Sunday night. 'I hope this wasn't a bad idea,' Morgan muttered at Laleh as he steered her to the door. 'Through to the back room,' he said.

Faces turned to look at them from the bar as they entered, and music was playing somewhere on a radio or juke-box. 'No food on Sunday,' the barman called to them as they walked through past the bar.

The inner room was used for pizzas, pool, parties and, judging by the graffiti on the wall, some pretty wild politics.

Firuze was standing by a table at the far end of the room, still in the simple dress she'd had on in the allotment that afternoon. She looked at Morgan, then at Laleh, and turned away through the door behind her.

'I leave you in here and wait out the back,' said Morgan. 'That's the agreement. If anything happens to Shaheenee there's someone out there with a gun on me. When you've finished talking, you go out the front and I join you there.'

Laleh nodded. She was frightened: for herself; for Morgan; for Shaheenee. She touched Morgan's arm. 'Thank you.'

The courtyard at the back was half-paved, and lined with crates of empty bottles, an ancient fig tree and a chicken run. It was over-looked by old apartment blocks behind.

'*You're to stay in the courtyard*,' the girl had said in her brief and precise instructions.

Morgan looked up at the balcony walkways above.

No way of telling here where the bloody gun was. He heard singing from the bar; he heard the girl whistle a call; he heard the answering call from a balcony above. He glimpsed the girl for a moment as a small door opened in a gateway at the end of a long archway down one side of the *osteria*. An elderly man stepped, stooping, through the doorway. He was dressed in a shabby lightweight suit and an old-fashioned white hat. Shaheenee had arrived.

Unseen by any of them, a white Mercedes stopped on the canal bank, backing slowly down the alley past the entrance to the *osteria*, its lights going out as it parked in the shadows beyond: a Swiss registration number, and black glass obscuring the interior and the face in the passenger seat – the Arab whose passport Morgan was carrying in an inside pocket. The killer.

PART FIVE

'Destination Hell . . .'

1

Morgan had spotted the gun in one corner of the long first-floor balcony, the barrel catching the light for a moment as Firuze opened the door for Shaheenee.

Inside, Morgan could see Laleh turn to face Shaheenee as he stepped into the room; he saw her speak and Shaheenee take off his hat and shake hands; and saw Firuze returning to the courtyard outside.

Morgan moved towards her as she reappeared, but heard the barrel of the gun rap the balcony railing above. A warning. He froze.

'You should keep Shaheenee inside,' he said in a low voice across the courtyard. 'He's safer in a crowd.'

The girl turned to look at him with her grave careful eyes. Morgan saw the gun move above him, the barrel turn towards him. He looked across at the girl and realized suddenly how very frightened she was. Another door opened somewhere on a second-floor balcony, and a shaft of light crossed the gun again. Morgan looked up and saw a young boy holding a toy pistol.

The girl walked away down the tunnel of arch towards the small exterior door in the large wooden gate.

'It's just you and the kid upstairs, isn't it,' said Morgan.

In a doorway outside, unseen in the darkness, the Arab was pulling the black leather belt from his trousers.

A square of light opened and closed as the girl stepped into the street and out of Morgan's sight. He looked back at the windows of the *osteria*, moving until he could see Laleh and Shaheenee talking at a table.

The intention had been to persuade Shaheenee to come away with them. Instead, when Shaheenee stood up, the two of them were shaking hands and it seemed that Laleh's persuasion had not been successful.

One moment Shaheenee was there and the next moment he had gone. Morgan opened the door – Laleh was alone inside. She looked round at him: 'He said, if I really come from Parviz, I was to go back and tell him on no account to talk with the Americans.'

'Which way did he leave?' asked Morgan.

Laleh nodded at the second of the inner doors. 'Through the kitchen.'

Morgan walked Laleh towards the front, past the bar and into the alley, looking both ways for a sign of Shaheenee or the girl. And saw instead the white Mercedes parked in the shadows at the end of the alley. All the alarm bells were ringing suddenly in his head.

A taxi had pulled in off the canal bank, disgorging a noisy group of fashionable revellers come to slum fashionably in the *osteria*.

'When you called the embassy,' Morgan asked Laleh, 'did you tell them where you were?'

'I had to leave them a number, but I didn't tell them where I was.'

'And did they tell you where your husband is staying?' Morgan was steering her towards the taxi.

Laleh nodded, taking a piece of paper from her pocket on which she'd written the address. She clutched at Morgan's arm. 'What's happening?'

'Do you remember where Reg is waiting?'

Laleh nodded.

'Tell her to get down here.' Morgan read the address on the piece of paper and gave it back to her. 'Then you go and join your husband. You might tell him that both Shaheenee and Parviz are in extreme danger, and ask him whether the American right hand has any idea what its left hand is doing.' Morgan held open the taxi door and pushed Laleh inside.

'What's going on?' she asked.

'Porta Ticinese,' Morgan told the driver, and slammed the door shut. He had no time to be polite. He had to find the old man and the girl.

The old man was waiting for the girl under the tree in the courtyard.

The girl, both hands pulling at the black leather belt around her throat, was dying in the darkness of a doorway out in the alley.

The old man should have gone now, without waiting. Instead, he turned the other way under the arch back towards the alley and the canal, knocking over a bicycle in the darkness as he opened the low door in the gate.

An offshoot of the canal ran alongside the alley, a channelled stream, covered with a low roof and lined with sloping slabs of stone where the women had washed for four hundred years or more. The girl was floating there, face down in the water, when Morgan found her. Cold and sick with anger, he knelt on the stones to lift her out.

Shaheenee at that moment stepped through the door and saw Morgan raising her from the water. In his grief and his fear the old man panicked, snatching the bicycle he'd knocked over.

Morgan looked up from the body to see him ride past, the bicycle wobbling, old Shaheenee pedalling desperately.

'Get back inside!' Morgan shouted at him. 'Stay in the light! Stay with the crowd!' Morgan looked down. He was still kneeling, holding the girl in his arms. The little boy walked from the *osteria* and stood in front of him, staring at the body and the water draining off it. Behind the boy, the white Mercedes was moving past the *osteria* and out onto the canal bank to follow the bicycle.

Morgan looked up at the boy. 'I'm sorry,' he said, and laid the body down.

When Reg arrived two minutes later, she found the boy kneeling by the body, rocking to and fro. Morgan had disappeared.

A road bridge crossed the canal one hundred and fifty yards beyond the *osteria*. Morgan ran for a tram, and stood at the rear window as the tram clanked at speed down the far bank of the canal, overtaking first the Mercedes and then the bicycle on the other side. The Mercedes was cruising slowly and without lights, content it seemed, to wait. Morgan had guessed where Shaheenee was going but, by the time he'd left the tram and climbed the old iron lift-bridge, both bicycle and pursuing car had passed him.

Shaheenee was well aware of the car by the time he reached the allotment. Perhaps he had some crazy idea that by locking himself in he could somehow be safe. In the event, he didn't even have time to do that; both his hands were still groping through holes in the gate trying to thread padlock through chain as the Mercedes pulled up outside.

Shaheenee fled into the dark garden. The killer kicked open the gate to follow, picking up the hoe as he passed the patch where the old lady had been working that afternoon.

Shaheenee had run to hide in the tall maize. The killer followed, swinging the blade of the hoe to scythe down the maize row by row until he exposed the old man, crouched on the ground. The killer raised Shaheenee's head with the blade of the hoe under his chin, knocked him sideways with the handle and chopped the blade down on the back of his neck. Then he emptied Shaheenee's pockets and took money from his wallet to suggest a motive for the killing.

Morgan, still running towards them from the bridge, could see the Mercedes turning across the narrow road on the canal bank. He saw the killer reappear from the allotment, and ducked into the bushes at the side of the road as the headlights of the Mercedes swept towards and past him.

Cold and sick with anger once again, and once again too late, Morgan found Shaheenee, a bundle of bloodied rags in the broken maize.

2

Whether on foot or with Shaheenee's bicycle, Morgan had no thought of pursuit when he left the allotment. All he wanted was a telephone to issue the number and description of that white Mercedes. But as he cycled back towards the iron bridge, he saw the bright lights of the stationary Mercedes by the bridge three hundred yards ahead of him. As he drew nearer, the dark figure of the Arab killer left the car and crossed the canal by the lift-bridge. The car then motored slowly on, the reason for its unexpected stop now visible to Morgan – the blue flashing lights of a police road-block in the distance further up the canal.

Morgan on the bicycle watched the killer on the endless iron steps, up one side and down the other, hoping that the killer wasn't watching him. But then, no one had seen him follow them to the allotment. The killer had no reason to expect pursuit.

He was standing now at the tram stop on the far side. The rumble of a tram was growing from the distance as Morgan ditched the bike and ran as quietly as he could up and over the same bridge.

The killer had already boarded the tram by the time Morgan made the road on the other side, but the driver, seeing him run, kept the doors open. Morgan climbed on. The tram echoed as it rumbled on its way, empty but for the killer – and the unseen driver at the front. The killer was studying a street-plan folded in his hand.

He looked up and saw Morgan; Morgan kept one hand in a pocket as though holding a gun.

The killer, for the first time, had been caught off guard. He pushed his map into an inside pocket. Morgan sat down on the wooden bench seat opposite him, knee to knee across the aisle. Difficult to tell, he thought, which of us is the more apprehensive. How long before he guesses there is no gun in my pocket? How long before the tram begins to fill up on its journey towards the city centre? The man's eyes were as cold and dark and hard as any Morgan had ever seen, and they were watching him without expression or movement. Once, they flickered as the tram slowed, glancing over Morgan's shoulder across the canal. Morgan did not need to turn. He could see the lights and the cars reflected in the window behind the Arab – blue flashing lights of the police road-block on the other side of the canal and the white Mercedes being checked through. That'll be Reg who's called them out, Morgan thought. She's found the body of the girl.

The tram pulled up at a stop, the doors hissing open. The man's eyes flickered a second time at the open door. Morgan moved the hand in his pocket. The doors closed; the tram was still empty. Morgan leaned forward.

'I've been following your handiwork across half of Europe.' His voice was loud over the noise of the tram. 'You're either very highly motivated or very highly paid. But you're beginning to make mistakes.'

There was no change of expression in the Arab's face. No sign that he even understood what Morgan was saying.

'It was hardly necessary to kill the girl. And the old lady on the train last night – she was another mistake.' Morgan was searching his face for the slightest sign. 'The woman you were trying to kill is the wife of an American diplomat. Did you know that? Or has someone crossed some wires?'

There wasn't a flicker in that face. Just the animal

alertness and patience. One mistake, thought Morgan, and he'll kill me. He's beginning to be sure I have no gun.

The tram crossed the bridge. Another cluster of blue flashing lights, visible towards the *osteria*, were reflected with the line of street lamps in the dark water. Then they left the canal behind.

'Who's operating you? Who's putting you in the right place at the right time? Who told you we were on that train in Paris?'

The tram jerked to another stop: Porta Genova and the first of the inner ring roads. This time a handful of passengers did climb on at the back of the tram, franking their tickets in the machine. Morgan was not displeased to see them. He smiled at the Arab. 'Do you have a gun? You wouldn't have risked crossing the frontier with a gun. Difficult enough not having a passport. But you might have acquired a gun by now. That depends how much support you have here. Support is easy if it's well organized. *Are* you organized? You certainly had a car and a driver waiting for you.'

The tram had stopped again. Another handful of Sunday promenaders clambered on board.

'What are your points of reference?' asked Morgan. 'Telephone numbers? Bars? Hotel rooms?'

An old woman with an armful of flowers sat down on the bench next to the Arab. Something of a tight fit. The Arab stood up. Morgan stood with him, both of them hanging on straps, face to face.

As another group pushed down the car, the killer deliberately brushed up against Morgan – making finally sure there was no gun in that pocket. Morgan noticed the Arab had now turned to watch the nearside front of the tram, looking for a landmark. The Duomo, thought Morgan. He's planning to bail out somewhere in the centre; with a rendezvous marked, no doubt, on that map in his inside pocket. Morgan half-smiled again. 'Another couple of stops and we're in the middle of town. What do I do then? You'll hardly want me following you. Do I find a policeman and turn you in? Not without some opposition, I would guess.'

One of the other standing passengers was listening to Morgan with puzzled interest. Morgan turned to him with an exaggerated smile and the man looked away embarrassed. The Arab's eyes were still watching for his landmark.

'Tell me who's operating you,' said Morgan. 'I'm not concerned with who you are – Palestinian, Kurd, Armenian, Zionist – I'm not even concerned what favours you've been promised. I want to know *whose* dirty work you are doing. It's his face I want to see. His flag I want to identify.'

The tram had turned the corner from Via Torino into Via Orefici, the Duomo briefly visible across its piazza. Passengers were beginning to push past them towards the centre doors. Morgan was still watching those eyes, so cold and dark and hard. 'I wonder if you have understood a single word I have said.' The tram began to slow for the next stop. 'You shouldn't have killed that girl.'

Morgan looked round suddenly as though signalling to someone, and the Arab's eyes followed his. Morgan reached into his jacket for the map; the killer thumped one knee up hard into his crutch; Morgan's legs went from under him in waves of pain. He found himself on his hands on the ribbed rubber flooring watching the black cord jeans of the Arab disappear through the open centre doors down onto the pavement.

Morgan dragged himself on hands and knees towards the front door by the driver. He could hear nothing, but saw the door close – and was conscious of people pulling or being pulled away from him. They would think he was drunk or ill. The tram had started to move as he pulled himself to his feet by the partition behind the driver.

'*Mi devi aprire*,' he said to the driver in a voice that intended to shout but in fact barely whispered.

223

'*É ammalato*,' someone said from behind him down the tram. 'He's ill, he has to get off.'

The tram stopped, the door opened and Morgan fell out onto the pavement, bent double, trying to breathe. He knew he still had a chance. The city map had been unwinding in his head ever since he'd boarded the tram wondering where the killer intended to get off. Even half-conscious on the floor of the tram, he'd seen where the killer had climbed out; had even anticipated his intended direction – not the short and crowded arcade back to the cathedral square, but the darker arched entrance to the Piazza dei Mercanti. And Morgan, on all fours in the gutter, was facing the second arched and northern entrance to the same piazza. A small and closed medieval piazza with the loggia balcony from where they once called sentences of death. The Arab was crossing the piazza west to east along the southern side. Still bent double like a circus act, Morgan followed.

He was feeling his way. The Arab, knowing the rough direction from his memory of the map, skirted the outside of the cathedral square through the arches and the porticos and the back-streets, scarcely glancing back for a sign of pursuit, so confident was he that Morgan had not followed.

He's making for the Galleria, thought Morgan, as the great arched arcade opened up in front of them like the mouth of a whale. Morgan was forty, fifty yards behind the Arab. Then he lost him. Suddenly, in the well-lit Galleria he was no longer there. Morgan glimpsed him briefly down the dark adjacent side-street leading back to the piazza. But again, when Morgan followed, the Arab had disappeared.

Morgan walked out into the arcade, looking, without hope, both ways into the promenading crowd, then turned back and saw the brass-railed steps of the Diurno – the hole in the ground down which the Arab must have bolted. Bottled up?

It would take Morgan five or ten minutes to call official

support, and surely somewhere there was a back way out of that subterranean maze of public baths and toilets. An even more extraordinary piece of architecture and design than the cathedral itself, thought Mogan, as he pushed open the door at the foot of the steps: wood panelling; coloured marble; the perfumes of soap and steam; a corridor of bathrooms with an attendant waiting, towels over her arm; a barber partitioned off, only one chair in use on this Sunday evening; a pedicure on the other side, a girl sitting in attendance on one extended naked foot.

No sign of the Arab in the open sections. Morgan walked through the steam into the corridor, trying any door that was closed on either side. One of them swung open to reveal an elderly army officer lying in a hot bath, his uniform laid out carefully on a chair. Morgan closed the door quickly on his shout of outrage. The attendant was calling at him. Morgan looked back, thinking suddenly of the one face he hadn't seen: the face at the end of that extended naked foot.

He was too late. He saw the Arab behind him through the steam, moving quickly to the exit, a second man hopping after him, carrying one shoe. Morgan ran from the far end of the corridor the full length of the Diurno, up the steps outside, back into the piazza. But the two of them had disappeared, swallowed up into the crowd.

Morgan returned back down the stairs into the subterranean palace, pulling open the curtain of the pedicure cubicle. The girl seemed almost to anticipate his questions.

'The Arab came in here,' she said. 'As soon as they saw you they both ran away.'

Morgan hardly needed a description from her. He picked up a *Daily American* from the table, an empty packet of Sweet Afton from the floor.

'Yes,' said the girl in reply to his next question. 'The American was fat and laughed a lot and made jokes in very bad Italian.'

3

Ashley was reading the menu to Blind Hugh in an equally atrocious Italian – 'Risotto, Tortellini, Ravioli, Minestrone, Spaghetti – '

'You can cut out the spaghetti, Ashley,' Hugh growled. 'Unless you want to spoonfeed me.'

Ashley could see Cal at the entrance, a little breathless as he checked his coat with the girl.

'Sorry if I kept you waiting,' Cal said as he joined them.

'It's Cal, Hugh,' Ashley murmured in the blind man's ear.

'Of course it's Cal,' replied Hugh impatiently.

'I had some calls to make,' said Cal. 'Organization and administration.'

Ashley pushed a piece of paper across the table at him. 'The janitor left a message.'

'He telephoned,' growled Hugh. 'Someone waits for you back at the ranch. Weren't you at the ranch?'

The 'ranch' was a rather beautiful seventeenth-century palace in the middle of Milan – what the State Department liked to call a hospitality house, though the funds for its upkeep came from another department.

Laleh had been waiting in the porter's lodge for twenty minutes when Cal walked in.

'I rang the embassy,' she said. 'They gave me the address.' The coldness in her voice checked Cal.

226

'I was told you were at the university,' he said.

'Oh?'

'Oh what?'

'I only left a telephone number,' said Laleh. 'I didn't say *where* I was.'

'Well' – Cal shrugged – 'I imagine someone figured it out. How come the sudden trip to Italy?'

'How come yours? I was *asked* to come.'

'By whom?'

'Parviz Vaziree. Morgan came with me.'

'Morgan?'

'My bodyguard.' Laleh was watching him. 'Sasan is dead.'

Cal nodded. 'I know.'

'I saw the men who killed him. They tried to kill *me* last night.'

Cal stared at her. 'What?'

'I want to know what's going on, Cal.'

'You *know* what's going on. I'm here to meet with Parviz and Shaheenee.' Cal shook his head, trying to follow what Laleh had been saying. 'What do you mean, they tried to kill you?'

Laleh looked round at the dark courtyard beyond the lodge. She shivered. 'Who else is here?'

'Hugh. Ashley Buchanan. We're eating round the corner – if you'd like to join us.'

'And the daughter?'

'She was asked not to come.' Cal took Laleh's arm. '*Who* tried to kill you?'

'I've been talking with Shaheenee,' said Laleh.

'*You've* been talking with Shaheenee? We haven't even managed to make contact with him yet.'

'He's very frightened,' said Laleh. 'He won't come out to talk with you. Nor does he want Parviz to talk with you.'

Cal gripped her arm. 'Will you tell me what happened to you?'

'I saw the men who killed Sasan. And Farshid. And

an old lady on the train last night, because they thought it was me.' Laleh drew her arm away. 'They're Palestinians – working for the CIA.'

'That's nonsense,' snapped Cal. 'You know that's nonsense.'

'You tell me what's real.'

'This bodyguard, this Morgan – was he with you?'

'He caught one of them.' Laleh watched her husband for a moment, then turned away.

'I have no idea what is going on, Lal. You have to believe that.'

'I'm tired.'

Cal nodded at the old janitor watching them from his own little inner office. 'Will you take my wife's bag upstairs and ask the housekeeper to move me into a double room.'

'That's all right.' Laleh turned her back on Cal. 'I'd rather be on my own if you don't mind.'

4

A large white motor caravan was driving out of the city on the *superstrada* northwards past Monza, the Arab staring through the windscreen beyond the driver at lines of headlights on the other carriageway, an endless stream of cars pouring back into the city.

They'd already passed a couple of bonfires, but now pulled off the road into a lay-by where a third fire of boxes and old tyres was blazing flame and black smoke. A young girl was standing beside it in the shortest of mini-skirts, her neat young body silhouetted against the flame. She turned to look at the mobile home, wondering if she had a client as it bumped over the rough ground past her, engine and lights cutting out when it stopped.

'Do you go with women, Geronimo?' Roundie climbed out of the driving seat with a chuckle, watching the girl's tentative approach. He pulled down the window. 'Go home to your Mummy,' he shouted at her, genuinely shocked at the girl's lack of age.

He walked up the interior of the caravan to the table, grinning as he listened to what the girl outside was telling him to do with his 'diseased appendage'.

'You've been making mistakes, Geronimo.' Roundie opened a bag and chucked a bundle of cloth at the Arab. 'You can forget accidents and natural causes and suicides. You don't have time any more.' He pulled a motorcycle crash-helmet from the bag and set it on the table. 'Hide inside the bubble,' said Roundie. 'They'll have your face painted all over Milan by the morning.'

The killer was unrolling his bundle of rag – an automatic pistol and a fat silencer.

'You do *not* try,' said Roundie, 'to kill the wives of senior American diplomats. You should have gone for the man. She wouldn't have known what to do without him.' Roundie lit up a Sweet Afton and drew on it. Compared to his usual bonhomie, he was jumpy, almost irritable. 'Now that son of a bitch is getting too damn close. I don't want him smelling the colour of my ass.' Roundie looked at the gun. 'No time for any more mistakes.'

The Arab was staring at him.

'I know, I know,' said Roundie, 'I should pull you out. I'm breaking all the rules. Your face is up in lights; you don't have papers and you don't have a passport. Well *I* don't have time, Geronimo. Where would I get a replacement flown in from?'

The killer had slid the weapon into his jacket, easing it in, easing it out.

'You'll have good back-up. You don't have to worry. I've found a racing driver.' Roundie sat down at the table and tapped the Arab's arm. 'Anyway, you're very good. Very dedicated. I'm gonna tell your people that.'

Headlights lit up one side of the caravan. A heavy truck pulled in by the bonfire. The mini-skirt walked over. The driver wound down his window. Whatever the haggle and whatever the price, the girl eventually walked round the front of the cab to climb in the far side.

'Italians!' said Roundie in disgust. 'That girl's not a day over fifteen!'

The truck pulled back onto the road.

'Kick her fire out, Geronimo.'

Dumb-fuck Arab, thought Roundie, as he watched the killer walk to the fire and kick it to pieces, a blaze of sparks in the late summer night.

5

Morgan had been burning wires all evening, telephones and telex, using, as Elgin had suggested, the honourable and democratic institutions of law and order. Not that they proved to be very responsive. The name Ralph Curtiss drew a blank in Rome, Berne, Wiesbaden and Vienna. Morgan had already checked out London and Paris, while New York confirmed Panmeridian Press as a legitimate agency, and Ralph Curtiss as a regular freelance on their books. Roundie's tracks, wherever they led from, were well covered.

Elgin was, as usual, unavailable, though the switchboard proved less guarded than usual. 'I'm calling from Milan,' Morgan had said.

'Oh,' the girl replied. 'Is that Mr Assuntino?'

Morgan was silent for a moment, surprised. 'Yes,' he lied.

'Mr Elgin,' volunteered the girl, 'left for the station an hour ago.'

The 23.49 out of the Gare de Lyon, thought Morgan, looking at his watch, the little wheels of paranoia turning again. He rang Assuntino's old home number, hoping the *magistrato* had not moved house in the intervening five years. His ever-apprehensive wife recognized Morgan's voice with reluctance and still more apprehension. 'Bob' was sleeping in Domodossola tonight, she told him.

And Elgin was arriving there, Morgan guessed, at 08.49 tomorrow morning.

He rang Reg – the fifth or sixth time he'd tried that evening. 'Piss off,' she said when she heard his voice. 'I've just got in the door and out of my clothes.' Four hours she'd been with the police at the *osteria*, she told him. 'When they catch up with you, I hope they break your head.'

It was past half past one when Morgan crawled out of a taxi and up the stairs into her two-room flat near the station, his mind and body trying to give up the struggle after three sleepless nights. He grinned at her scowling face. They had once shared a week of sleepless nights in a stake-out waiting for a terrorist who'd never turned up to claim his cache of arms and explosives. They were used to keeping themselves awake, laughing or scowling.

Reg sat him at the kitchen table with a bottle of wine and warmed up a pan of pasta and beans while they both debriefed each other: Morgan recounted the deaths of the girl and Shaheenee and his ride in the tram with the killer; Reg, her evening with the police and the bodies. Reg had taken photocopies of the Arab's face from the passport. Hopefully by the morning every policeman in Milan would have seen the picture.

'Can you pull anyone private in?' asked Morgan. 'A couple or three with four wheels and a brain?'

'What do I tell them?'

'If they're your colour, Reg, tell them we're chasing the CIA.'

'Are we?'

'I don't know.' Morgan looked up at her. 'I shall want the fat man's laughing head on a plate if it is. His balls in my teeth.'

She gave him his *pasta fagioli* with the pepper-mill and the olive oil, and sat across the table from him: 'I haven't seen you angry like this for five years.' She laughed as she watched him eat. 'It's good for you.'

*

Reg fed and watered him, lent him her bathroom and, scowling again, drove him, at four in the morning, to the station at Porta Garibaldi to pick up the night train from Rome to Geneva.

Morgan stretched out in an empty first-class compartment for the couple of hours' sleep that would keep him going through one more day.

It was already dawn when he walked out into the empty streets of Domodossola, cool under the mountains. He drank a pint of coffee as soon as the first bar opened and sat outside the station waiting for the first taxi.

Assuntino's hotel was halfway up the mountain at a little spa resort – cedar-tree gardens dating back to the 1920s and a 'grand' hotel of Marienbad pretensions in creaking pine with fading carpets. Assuntino, the only inmate under sixty, laughed when he saw Morgan walking into the solemn ritual of breakfast.

They drove together up the valley, zigzagging higher into the hills, to find Veltri's village of exile already deserted by the able-bodied this Monday morning. The children played football in the piazza, a few grandparents lined up wizened in the sun.

One of Veltri's bodyguards monitored the arrival of Morgan and Assuntino. He was watching from the wooden balcony of Veltri's house of exile, shouting coaching tips in Neapolitan dialect as Morgan joined the game of football. Veltri, it seemed, was off with the other bodyguard, high in the larch and the pine looking for wild mushrooms.

By the time Elgin made his appearance, Veltri had returned, laying out his 'catch' at one of the bar tables – *edulis, badius* and *scaber* – and Morgan was still playing football. Assuntino, like the older men, sat on the sunny side of the piazza as the early-morning bus hooted its double-note progress through the hairpins in the valley and up into the village. A distinguished, if portly, English gentleman climbed off.

Typical of Elgin, thought Morgan, to grudge the fifteen dollars for a taxi and keep them all waiting an extra half-hour.

They sat with Veltri and his fungi on the terrace, Elgin wondering if the bar would run to tea and toast and Oxford Marmalade, Veltri watching him with apprehension. Assuntino introduced Elgin as '*le patron* from Paris'.

'You are the man who hunts me down?' asked Veltri.

Elgin shook his head. 'The initial evidence against you was not supplied by Interpol. It came from Italy through Mr Assuntino.'

The *magistrato* corrected him. 'It came from outside.'

'Wherever that may be.' Elgin fixed Veltri with his interrogator's eyes. 'Whatever its source, the evidence appeared exactly ten days after you, Mr Veltri, had returned from a business trip to Moscow. Perhaps it would be helpful to know the purpose of that trip?'

Veltri, watching his interrogator's eyes, looked away.

Elgin picked up one of the fungi. '*Boletus edulis*,' he said. 'Known to us in the UK as the "penny bun mushroom". The French go mad about them. Die in their dozens every year picking the wrong ones.' He smelt it and replaced it. 'Whatever happened on that trip in Russia seems to have set off a train of events which has caused the death of three exiled politicians.'

'Three?' Veltri looked round at Morgan.

'Shaheenee was killed last night,' said Morgan.

Veltri stared at him.

The woman from the bar carried out their tray – a cup of tea, packeted toast, three coffees and a bottle of grappa, which she poured liberally into the coffees.

Elgin was watching Veltri. 'You made an agreement with the Russians on Shaheenee's behalf, with the blessing of Sasan and Farshid. Now all three are dead. What was the agreement?'

'*Un accordo politico o commerciale?*' asked Assuntino.

'An agreement of patronage.'

'Shaheenee's party is helped to power, over a period of years,' suggested Elgin, 'in return for neutrality over Afghanistan, a low religious profile and a three-way oil deal, you being the third party.'

'I think you make an oversimplification – '

Elgin gestured in the air. 'Broad strokes,' he said. 'That was the general framework of the agreement.'

Morgan intervened: 'And if Parviz Vaziree survives? The agreement would still be valid?'

'*If* Parviz agrees to accept the Russians. He and his father always opposed any form of outside influence.'

'Today he's talking to the Americans.'

Veltri looked surprised.

Elgin sipped at his tea with distaste. 'As a representative of Interpol, I am in Italy to inform the Italian authorities' – he gestured at Assuntino – 'that the evidence channelled through us and against you cannot be substantiated and seems to have been a plant. The only hard evidence concerns – ' Elgin looked at Morgan, cueing him in.

'The passage of money through Swiss banks in Lugano,' said Morgan. 'Laundering.'

'Your only crime in that respect,' said Assuntino, 'is non-payment of Italian taxes. At a rough calculation one and a half million dollars.'

'I am free?' asked Veltri.

'You pay the one-and-a-half million dollars to the tax office in Geneva and you are free to go home.'

Veltri gestured round at the grey stone buildings and the mountains. 'And where am I going to find one-and-a-half million dollars? Picking mushrooms?'

Elgin sipped again at his tea, pausing in horror to lift a tea-bag out of the cup. 'Can nobody in this country make a decent cup of English tea?' He broke open the noisy Cellophane pack of toast. Veltri stared at him. Elgin had one more surprise for them, as he munched his toast – a photograph he took from his inside pocket and laid on the table; a younger, but unmistakable

Roundie. Elgin looked at Assuntino. 'You know this man?'

Assuntino hesitated, then nodded.

'He came to you with information about Mr Veltri?'

Assuntino nodded again.

'When?' asked Morgan in surprise.

'In Birmingham. He had information that persuaded Mr Veltri to accept extradition from England.'

Morgan picked up the photograph and turned it over. There was a number and code on the back. He looked round at Elgin. 'Find it on a tram in Guatemala, did you?'

Elgin ignored the coldness and anger in Morgan's jibe and turned instead to Veltri. 'Do *you* know this man?'

'He's a journalist,' replied Veltri. 'Mr Ralph Curtiss, Panmeridian Press. He's also an agent of the CIA and has been for fifteen years.'

Morgan looked at Elgin. Elgin didn't seem in the least surprised.

Veltri stood up. 'There was a girl with Shaheenee.'

'She's dead,' said Morgan.

Veltri looked away. He seemed suddenly shocked – on the verge of tears.

'Who was she?' asked Morgan.

'His grand-daughter.'

Elgin was fiddling again with the Cellophane pack of toast. Veltri reached over the table and snatched it away from him, crushing it in his hand and throwing it at him. 'Eat your toast! Eat your English toast!' He turned on his heels and walked away.

An astonished Elgin watched him go. 'Funny sort of a chap,' he said, and turned to Morgan. 'I don't expect you to believe me, but the photograph of Mr Curtiss only arrived in the office yesterday. Flown over from Nicaragua. Someone who knew Mr Curtiss in Chile. It seems Mr Curtiss was working in Santiago in 1972 and 1973. Engineering a scoop on the fall of Allende, perhaps.'

Morgan stood up from the table.

'We can't touch him, Morgan,' warned Elgin. 'Not unless he actually breaks the law himself, and people like that are usually very careful not to.'

6

Annie had arrived in Milan early that morning, hungry and thirsty and dirty from a night on the train.

Her Byzantine friends had organized a welcome: one man in a heavy dark suit by one of the fountains outside the station, carrying a raincoat and looking very hot in the sunshine. He couldn't have seemed more obvious if he'd been wearing a fur hat. But he spoke good English, knew why Annie had come and understood perfectly all her physical needs: first coffee and brioches at one of the open-air bars; then a bathroom in the Diurno under the station while he waited for her in his car; and finally a telephone to check any message her father might have left for her at the consulate.

Dear Daddy, thought Annie, quite sure now he was playing both ends against the middle, for he'd managed to leave her the exact address of the American 'hospitality' house where the meeting with Parviz was to take place. 'It is also conceivable,' he'd written, 'that we will break for lunch in a restaurant called the Bagutta.'

The Russian smiled when he saw the address of the hospitality house. 'An American safe house,' he said. 'Except everyone knows about it. You'll have trouble getting beyond the gate.'

Morgan was past being surprised by anything or anyone, even Annie's presence in that Milan street, sitting on the pavement, her back to the wall, ignoring him as he climbed out of Reg's Alfa and crossed the road.

The iron gate inside the arch was locked, the house itself a seventeenth-century palace built around a court-yard. Dorff was sitting with his back to the wall at the far side, head cocked up at the sun. He hauled himself to his feet when he saw Morgan through the gate and strolled over. 'Are you official, Joe?'

'No.'

Dorff smiled. 'Then you can't come in, can you. You're on leave. You're not even here.'

Morgan returned to the street and sat down on the pavement next to Annie. 'Very selective, this American hospitality,' he said. He looked round at her. 'Annabel Buchanan, born 1949.'

'Haven't we been through this before?'

'We weren't on the same side before.'

Annie glanced round at him. 'Whose side are we on now, then?'

'On the side of making sure Parviz Vaziree stays alive. It is becoming quite a struggle to keep any of them alive.'

Annie was watching him, anticipating what he was about to say.

'They killed Shaheenee last night. And his grand-daughter.' Morgan nodded over his shoulder at the archway and the iron gate. 'They don't yet know that in there.'

Morgan turned his head to look at Annie. She was crying – streaming tears without a sound. She dropped her head into her hands, and two elegant Milanese ladies looked at her as they passed, curious at her grief.

'Some years ago,' said Morgan quietly, 'you decided that the future of Vaziree and their party was best served by Moscow. The Russians plugged you into Veltri; you plugged Veltri into Vaziree and Shaheenee, but unfortunately old Vaziree would have nothing of it. Until of course he was rather conveniently assassinated.'

Morgan felt Annie stiffen beside him. 'Don't worry, Miss Buchanan, I have no official brief to investigate the assassination of Parviz's father, nor to investigate your connections, official, or otherwise, with the Russians. Interpol is not a political organization.'

A car pulled into the end of the street and parked with two wheels up on the pavement: a white Mercedes with dark glass and a Geneva registration.

'How did Shaheen and Firuze die?' whispered Annie.

'Firuze?'

'His grand-daughter.'

'She was very beautiful.'

Annie looked away, tears streaming again.

'They did not die gently.'

Morgan hauled himself to his feet and walked up the street towards the Mercedes. No Arab. Only Roundie in the driving seat grinning at Morgan. 'Mr Hunter-Brown – '

Morgan took last night's crumpled pack of Sweet Afton from his pocket and tossed it in the open window: 'You leave too much of your litter lying around, Mr Curtiss.'

7

The night before, Parviz had made his first attempt to escape, waiting till Dorff was asleep, then opening the balcony door and contemplating the dangers of trying to swing himself down onto the balcony one floor below. Dorff had woken to find him tying his sheets together – and had then spent a sleepless night 'on guard', since his bed could only cover one of the two doors. Prisoner and keeper were both at the end of their tethers by the time their Italian police escort had delivered them to the Americans in the morning.

Laleh had been waiting for Parviz. She slipped down to the courtyard as soon as his car pulled in through the gate. 'I've seen Shaheenee,' she told him. 'His only one message was to beg you not to talk with the Americans.'

'Where is he?'

'Here in the city. He is very frightened.'

'We are all frightened.' Parviz looked round at the approach of Cal and Ashley. 'What do they want from me?'

Two hours later, having listened to an endless lecture on the economy, politics and sociology of his country, Parviz was none the wiser. He knew that Sasan, Shaheenee and Farshid had made contact, if not an agreement, with the Russians, and he assumed that the Americans were anxious to forestall any such agreement. Whether they were actually offering something in its place was more difficult to determine, even for Laleh, interpreting across the table for him when he chose to speak in Farsi.

'Your country is ready for a measured amount of freedom,' said Blind Hugh. 'But lacks the wherewithal to create it. Your country has long traditions.'

'My country,' said Parviz, 'is tired.' His voice was suddenly angry. 'Tired of a war it does not need; tired of a fanaticism it never chose; tired of priests and prophets.' He looked at Ashley. 'Tired of the British.' He looked at Cal. 'Tired of the Americans. Tired of the Russians. Tired of the oil companies. It seems we can never move without the dirty help of someone else.' Parviz stood up. 'Last time it was money to fund strikes and acts of terrorism. Destabilization. I imagine the pattern will be the same next time. Except next time *we* will decide the outcome ourselves. The end *and* the means.'

Laleh looked down at the table, moved by what he had said and the passion with which he had expressed it.

'I can assure you,' said Cal, 'we are all in search of the democratic solution.' He shuffled his papers together and stood up. 'I suggest we break for lunch. We have a table booked round the corner.'

'No reason for despair yet,' Ashley murmured, as Parviz walked past him out of the door. 'Washington always takes its time.'

Parviz heard a fountain through the open windows of the corridor where the plain-clothes man was waiting. He looked out, and Annie's shout cut across the sunshine and shadow in the courtyard below.

'Parviz Vaziree!'

She'd started shouting the moment she saw him.

'Parviz Vaziree! Shaheen is dead!'

Parviz could see Annie across the courtyard at the locked iron gate in the archway that led to the street.

'They've murdered Shaheen Shaheenee!'

Laleh heard Annie from inside the conference room.

242

Ashley had led Blind Hugh out and she was alone at the table with Cal. She looked up at him in shock. Cal was also frozen as he listened to the girl shouting outside.

Annie switched into Farsi, one sentence shouted very deliberately.

'What's she saying?' asked Cal sharply.

Annie shouted again, repeating the words.

'What's the girl saying out there, Lal?'

Laleh looked at her husband and turned to the door. 'I can't hear what she's saying,' she lied, and walked past him out of the room.

8

Morgan had known the restaurant for nearly forty years. His father had introduced him to it when they returned to Milan with Rudi to lay the ghosts of war. Three generations of the Pepori had watched him through their doors with welcome or apprehension, Signora Bianca feeding him in their side room when he was alone, adopting Reg as a Baguttiana, even remembering Morgan's father all those years ago with his own memories from the days before the war. It wasn't too difficult to persuade them now to let him unbolt the bars from the toilet window in the inner courtyard. A practical joke, Morgan had said – though Mario and Adriano knew him too well to believe a word of it.

The American table was in the Artists' Room where the walls were covered in paintings, with modern frescoes above and on the ceiling. Laleh, Blind Hugh, Ashley, Cal and Parviz. Dorff and the plain-clothes Italian had been seated at a separate table.

Parviz waited until the first course arrived on Dorff's table and the German was tucking hungrily into his pasta. Parviz, with a muttered apology, stood up and walked to the door of the toilets. Only Laleh knew he was following the instructions shouted at him by Annie from the street.

Dorff watched him go, snatching one more mouthful of pasta before following him. *The far door*, Annie had shouted. Parviz pushed it open. Morgan was standing inside. He pulled Parviz in and locked the door. 'You

244

go through the window,' he said. 'She's waiting for you with a taxi out in the street.'

Parviz stared at him.

'It's your choice. A shouted message isn't much to go on.'

Parviz shook his head. 'Why should you want to help me?'

'You asked for political asylum in my country. This is the best I can offer – in another country and without guarantees.'

The main door outside opened and closed. Still Parviz hesitated. Dorff's voice called over the partition. 'You finished in there, Garibaldi?'

The sneer in that German voice seemed to decide Parviz. He climbed onto the toilet, up onto the window ledge. Morgan flushed the WC to cover the sound and Parviz dropped to the ground outside.

'What you need is another three years' chick-peas in your bowels,' called Dorff. 'Roughage.' He knocked impatiently at the door. 'Come on, buddy-boy. My dinner's getting cold.'

Morgan unbolted the door and pulled it open. Dorff's mouth gaped as he saw him.

'It's all right, buddy-boy,' said Morgan. 'I'm unofficial. I'm on leave. I'm not even here.'

The taxi door was open, the engine running. The driver pulled away as soon as Parviz had stumbled into the back seat next to Annie. Dorff and the plain-clothes man came chasing from the restaurant, and a white Mercedes pulled out fifty yards beyond, accelerating down the narrow street in pursuit of the taxi. Reg was waiting in her Alfa. She pulled across to block the road once the taxi had passed. Roundie, in the Mercedes, slewed to a sideways halt, blasting on his airhorns. At which moment, Cal and Ashley also came hurrying from the restaurant. Cal turned to stare in surprise when he realized who it was in the Mercedes. Holy cow; unholy stranger.

*
245

Back inside the restaurant, Morgan walked out of the toilet and came face to face with Laleh, who was still sitting at the table with Blind Hugh. 'What's happening?' Hugh was asking. 'Will someone tell me what is happening?'

Laleh was looking at Morgan. 'It was my fault,' she said. 'Leaving the telephone number with the embassy.' Shaheenee's death, she meant.

Blind Hugh's hands were feeling over the table trying to find Laleh. 'Will someone tell me what is happening?'

'You have a wild card in your pack, blind man,' said Morgan. Hugh turned his face from one side to the other, trying to sense the direction of Morgan's voice.

Morgan was looking at Laleh. 'A Mr Ralph Curtiss, otherwise known as Roundie, operating for the Central Intelligence Agency.'

9

The house even looked Byzantine – someone's miniature suburban folly of a hundred or so years ago, the exterior walls decorated with Greek and Roman inscriptions and pieces of frieze, a tree-filled garden behind a wall, and a woman dressed like a Georgian peasant who unlocked the gate and led them upstairs into a formal and mirrored sitting room. Apart from her, the house seemed empty and very silent. She left them alone.

'It seems they did not expect me to come,' said Parviz.

'They did not know.' Annie looked round the room. 'All they said was "the door is still open if they want to walk in".'

'With Veltri?'

'With Veltri.' Annie touched Parviz on one arm and spoke in a low voice. 'I think it best we do not yet tell them Shaheenee is dead.'

Parviz sat down. 'I should have killed myself in prison years ago. I tried to pretend to myself that I was still alive because I was important. But I knew all the time they were keeping me alive for a purpose of their own. They have used me as an instrument of death. I am as guilty as the killer himself.'

'That's nonsense,' said Annie. 'You know it's nonsense.'

Parviz looked up at her. 'Who is the killer?'

'They say he's an Arab.'

Parviz's laugh was short, ironic and sad. 'We are all of us Arabs. Aryans and Arabs. You tell me the difference. He spoke a line of verse in Arabic, the poem the Baha'i boy had taught him.

The Singer sings about fire and strangers.
And the evening was evening
And the Singer was singing.

'Zap in and zap out,' said Blind Hugh. 'It's not an embassy. It has no immunity.'

'Wherever and whatever it is,' said Cal.

'Consulate, trade mission, Aeroflot – it could be any of them.'

'Whichever it turns out to be,' said Ashley, 'I'm sure the Italians would rather we avoided physical confrontation on their sovereign territory.'

'Sovereign, hell!' said Hugh. 'We have a dozen missile and radar bases within two hundred miles of here. We'll call it security.' The zapping, he meant.

Laleh watched him in disbelief from the far end of the room. The four of them had returned to the conference room, lunch cut short before it even began.

When the porter called up to say a Mr Ralph Curtiss had arrived, it was Hugh who insisted he was shown upstairs.

'Does he have authorization?' asked Cal.

'Knock it off, Cal. We're not playing games any more. On the chessboard you just lost us a Middle East bishop.'

Roundie walked in with an address written on a sheet of paper, and a cursory nod for all of them. 'Moscow has a quiet house it uses,' he said. 'Not as grand as this place, but it serves the same purpose.' He laid the sheet of paper on the table in front of Laleh. 'I think Mrs Colraine should try and talk him out.' He looked at Laleh. 'For his own safety.'

'Just what the hell is your role in all of this?' she asked.

'My role is irrelevant to our problem at the moment. What is relevant is that one of us should have a hand to play with the Russians.' Roundie looked at Ashley.

'I think that means you and your oil companies, Mr Buchanan.' He pushed the telephone across the table at him. 'I'll be your dummy hand.'

The telephone rang in the deserted piazza. The village priest eventually appeared from the church to pull open the kiosk door and answer.

The afternoon was grey and damp in the mountains; thunder was rolling somewhere further east, the priest guessed, as he tucked up his cassock and climbed the hill. In common with most in the village, the priest had taken a liking to their obligatory guest, a generous rogue buying drinks and favours at the bar. The priest stopped halfway up the steps and shouted for him. 'Telephone for Mr Veltri.'

By the time Veltri had walked down to the pay-phone, Ashley had been listening to ten minutes of silence punctuated only by the striking of the village clock. 'Ashley Buchanan,' he said, when asked by Veltri to repeat his name. 'I am authorized to negotiate on behalf of a major oil company which wishes to remain anonymous.'

Veltri was looking out across the valley at a dusting of snow on the peaks to the east. He'd already guessed what this Buchanan was about to say.

'The negotiation would be for the outright purchase of your oil refinery and the transfer of the leases on your oil-tankers. They are nothing but a financial embarrassment to you.'

'And why,' asked Veltri, 'should a major oil company wish to bail *me* out? Where is the hidden price?'

Back in the conference room, Ashley glanced up across the table at Roundie, who was listening on an extension. 'You are asked to communicate with your contact at the Russian Embassy and inform him that Shaheenee is dead and that the agreements made with him are no longer valid.'

Laleh was watching Ashley. The Englishman was

quite clearly unhappy about what he was saying to Veltri. Roundie had scribbled something on a piece of paper and pushed it across the table at him. Ashley read it, looked up at Roundie, then, even more reluctantly, read out what was written over the phone to Veltri:

'*Tell your contact that Parviz Vaziree spent the morning talking with the Americans.*'

Laleh turned on Cal. 'And you can stand there listening to that?'

'Would you really want Mr Vaziree riding home on a Russian tank?' replied Cal. 'Slap into the heart of the gulf oilfields?'

Laleh shook her head in disbelief as Ashley put the phone down. 'Do you realize what will happen to him?'

'He has protection,' said Ashley.

Laleh looked at Roundie. 'Does he have protection, Roundie?'

Roundie looked at Cal.

'Of course he has our protection,' said Cal. 'If you can bring him back.'

Laleh was still looking at Roundie.

Roundie shrugged. 'If the State Department says he has protection, he must have.'

Laleh took the sheet of paper on which Roundie had written the Russian address. She walked to the door. 'Ask Roundie how many people have been killed, Cal,' she said over her shoulder. 'The State Department doesn't seem to have protected anyone so far.'

Back in the mountains, Veltri was still standing in the pay-phone cabin, gazing across the valley at the first dusting of snow on the peaks. He took his black book of telephone numbers from an inside pocket and began to dial. It seemed to him he'd been offered not quite fortuitously a solution to all his problems – and yet it was with reluctance that he approached the call he was about to make.

10

Parviz and Annie had been joined by the dark-suited official who had met Annie at the station that morning. He walked in with a smile and a bottle of vodka, and a doomed attempt at jollity. Nothing he could do or say would raise Parviz from his despair or persuade him that the day's events were anything more than a desperate and undignified attempt to stay alive.

It was a relief to them all when the sound of a telephone summoned the Russian away to another room in the house. Not such a relief when Annie walked to the window and saw a familiar figure climbing from a taxi outside in the street: Laleh Colraine, ringing in vain at the gate, then stepping back into the road to look over the wall up at the house. She returned to the taxi and asked the driver to park and wait.

Parviz joined Annie at the window, and Laleh looked up at them from the street.

'If *she* knows we're here,' said Parviz, 'then everyone knows.'

He slumped down again into the armchair, watching Annie as she crossed the room to the door – and found it locked.

Annie turned to look at him, hoping he hadn't seen. His slight pale figure seemed to sag even further. Annie looked round the room in despair as though she might find something with which to raise his spirits. She walked over to him, took his arms and drew him to his feet, turning him towards the mirror.

'Stand up,' she said in Farsi. 'You are Parviz Vaziree, son of Vaziree – and you are the only one left alive.'

As though on cue, the mirror in front of them separated – a door that slid open – and a second Russian, altogether less welcoming, came in. He smiled for the sake of politeness and asked them to return tomorrow.

Parviz looked at him, then at Annie. 'Has it been understood,' he asked, 'that I am asking for protection?'

The Russian himself replied. 'These things take time.'

'I have no time,' said Parviz. 'I am a political prisoner. I am asking for asylum.'

'For that, it would be necessary to go to Rome. There is no immunity here.'

'And just how the hell,' exploded Annie, 'do you expect us to get ourselves alive and well to Rome?'

'In that case,' said the Russian, 'you come back tomorrow and we try to make another arrangement.'

Annie's voice was still raised. 'If you send him back out there into those streets, there isn't going to be a tomorrow.'

Laleh, hearing the house door open, crossed the street to the patterned iron gate. She saw Parviz and Annie walking out, and Annie turning in front of him to stop on the path under the trees.

Parviz was looking past Annie at Laleh behind the gate. 'She is American,' he said. 'I should be safe with her.'

'Stay here – they dare not touch us here,' implored Annie.

Parviz seemed to close his eyes. 'I am tired,' he said.

Annie clung to him, blocking the path.

'The way I am going to die,' he said, in a low voice, '*if* I am going to die, I would rather die among strangers.'

'You're going to be all right,' came Laleh's voice through the gate. 'You are protected.'

Annie turned on her: 'No one is protected!'

252

Parviz took Annie's face in his hands, repeated the refrain of the Arab poem the Baha'i boy had taught him in the prison camp:

And the evening was evening
And the Singer was singing.

He took her face in both hands and kissed her, then walked past her to the gate.

Annie heard the click of the gate being opened electronically from inside the house; the bang as it closed again; footsteps on the path behind her, the gentler of the two Russians, still hot in his heavy suit, concerned as he watched her slide down against a tree to sit in despair on the ground. He reached a hand down to her shoulder and she turned to snarl at him like a wild animal:

'Don't touch me!'

11

The taxi skirted the park, the afternoon sun hazy and heavy through the trees.

Laleh only said one thing, sitting next to him in the back seat: 'You have been manipulated. I am very sorry how everything has happened.' She looked out at the traffic towards the castle building up into a jam. 'We have all been manipulated.'

Parviz was trying to remember the rest of the poem, as though the Baha'i boy were there holding his hand, their roles reversed. 'The singer sings about fire and strangers, and they interrogate him, why do you sing? He replies – because I sing.'

Parviz could see the castle on one side, a bank of trees, a man astride a motorcycle against the sun at the top of the bank where surely there was no road, a second man in a crash helmet standing in front of it.

They searched within him but found only his heart.
They searched his heart but found only his people.

The second man was taking off his crash helmet and climbing onto the pillion of the motorbike. Parviz watched him and wondered.

They searched his voice but found only his sadness.
They searched his sadness but found only his prison.
They searched his prison but only found themselves in chains.

254

The motorbike was speeding down over the grass bank towards the road, but Parviz was no longer watching it.

'The Americans have a house,' Laleh was telling him. 'You'll be safe there.'

There were two lanes of traffic, stationary in either direction; the motorcycle cut across them towards their taxi.

'And the evening was evening,' Parviz recited in Arabic. 'And the singer was singing.' He could see children buying coloured balloons by the castle; a flower-stall in a blaze of colour; a circle of people round a half-naked man blowing fire from his mouth; an older man alone against the park railings seated on a stool playing a curious wailing music, flexing the vibrating blade of a saw. Every single image seemed unreal to Parviz, appearing in slow motion like a film running down.

The motorbike appeared in the gap between two cars in front of them, against the flow of traffic and braking to a standstill alongside the taxi. The pillion rider drew a gun from inside his leather jacket as he rose on his footrests to step off — an Arab, all dressed in black, whose eyes blazed with fear or fervour. He pushed the taxi-driver to one side and held the gun two-handed through the open window, his eyes on Parviz. Laleh shouted, and for a moment the Arab seemed to hesitate. Then deliberately, like the slaughterer with the bolt, he shot Parviz twice in the head and chest. Laleh felt something hit her as though the gun had sprayed warm oil over them, then saw the Arab's eyes and gun move for a moment onto her. She was covered up and cowering into the corner away from Parviz. The motorcyclist was now shouting, the bike revving in a scream. The Arab turned away.

The sequence of events that followed was later pieced together by police and journalists from astonished and terrified onlookers. The motorbike rose, like a horse on its back legs, taking off at speed before the Arab had

255

mounted. Its front wheel in the air, it raced down the gap between the two lines of traffic. The Arab flew off the back of the bike onto the road. The Arab picked himself up, gun still held in both hands, and swung round towards the other cars and the line of faces watching in blank amazement from a bus. The motorbike had gone.

As Laleh opened her eyes, she saw the Arab walk deliberately round the front of the taxi, gun pointing at them. He climbed into the front passenger seat of the taxi, holding the gun at the driver's head. One small gap had opened up across all three lines of traffic. The killer's gun prodded at the driver's cheek. The driver swung out into the gap, across three lines of traffic, up onto the sidewalk, through the stall of flowers, across the grass bank and back onto the road beyond. Laleh was conscious only of the noise and a curtain of flowers as they hit the stall. She turned her head to look back and saw the rear window obscured in a thick dark-coloured fluid, flecked in white; the same colour and substance was over her clothes and on her hands and face. She took her scarf and turned to Parviz to wipe him clean. There was a small neat hole in the centre of his forehead – but the back of his head seemed to have exploded open. She covered his face and staring eyes.

12

Some twenty minutes after the shooting, the taxi was found abandoned, with the body, on a wide and deserted roadway under the old arena at the opposite end of the park.

A cordon of *carabinieri* had sealed off the area by the time Morgan arrived. Dorff was already there, walking away from the taxi. 'He'd still be alive if you'd left him with me,' he said, angry and bitter at Morgan.

Morgan made no reply. For once, he thought, the German is probably quite correct. One of the *carabinieri* was drawing a chalk cirle round Laleh's bloodstained scarf on the ground.

'The woman and the taxi–driver are still with him,' said the officer in charge, looking at Morgan's ID card. 'Hostages. Apparently there was a motor caravan parked here. He took them with him – with a gun.'

Morgan walked round the car. Parviz's face seemed to stare at him from the back seat, illuminated in flashes, like a neon sign, as the police photographer took pictures.

Another official car had pulled up – Assuntino, with Elgin in the back. And behind them, cruising slowly to a halt under the arena wall, the white Mercedes with the darkened glass and the Swiss registration number – the ultimate arrogance as Roundie climbed out and stood by the car to watch the scene from outside the cordon. Wondering, thought Morgan, where the hell the Arab has taken Mrs Laleh Colraine.

Morgan looked back at Reg in her Alfa and she indicted with a nod that, yes, she'd seen the Merc.

Elgin wound down his window as Morgan passed. He too was watching Roundie. 'Every card we have played,' he said to Morgan, 'has been marked and dealt by that man. But constitutionally and legally neither you nor I can touch him. And I would advise you not to try.' He raised his voice slightly as Morgan walked away. 'The case is over, Morgan. The file is closed.'

Morgan watched Cal arrive and walk, looking pale, to the abandoned taxi. He stopped short when he saw Laleh's bloodstained scarf in its chalk circle. As he stooped to it, he was restrained by the senior *carabiniere*. The quiet, greying American talked to the *carabiniere* for two or three minutes – then turned and noticed Roundie by the Mercedes, beyond the cordon.

Morgan walked far enough towards them as they met to hear their voices.

'If anything's happened to my wife,' said Cal. 'I'll hound you and your whole organization through every congressional committee in Washington.'

'Don't come the injured innocent with me, Cal.' The joking smile was there as always, but the voice was cold and despising. 'You Ivy League boys setting the world to rights – forgetting it was you who made us your instruments in the first place.'

'I think you forget sometimes what principles you're meant to be working for.'

Roundie laughed without humour. 'The Stars and Stripes for ever, Cal. Saving the free world from too much freedom.' Roundie looked beyond Cal at Morgan. 'We're all democrats at heart. But in the real world, some of us can no longer believe it in the head.'

Parviz's shattered head was strapped with a rubber bandage as the *carabinieri* pulled a screen around the car and eased the cold and stiffening body out of the abandoned taxi onto a rubber sheet.

13

Reg had recruited Toni — comrade from her past, a terrorist she had sheltered instead of shopped. An academic and an artist he was nonetheless quick, careful and well organized. He'd gathered in another pair of drivers, three cars with radio telephones and a walkie-talkie for Reg — four cars alternating to keep track of that white Swiss Mercedes.

Roundie knew well enough he was being tailed — by Reg and Morgan in the car he recognized. What he didn't realize was the alternating sequence of the other three cars, always straddling him to front and rear. When he blasted suddenly across a pair of red lights to lose Reg and Morgan, he believed himself clear.

It was Reg who guessed his intention as they kept in contact with Toni over the walkie-talkie. Roundie had circled half the outer ring road, and half the *tangenziale*, to exit more or less where he'd started, north of the Viale Zara onto the Lecco *superstrada*. At the Monza roundabout he turned down the boulevard towards the Royal Palace and parked on the verge a couple of hundred yards short of the palace gates.

'If he's picking up the Arab,' said Reg, 'he'll make for the Splügen. A handful of men with toy guns on the top of the mountains. That's the border crossing I'd go for if I didn't have a passport.'

'*If* he's picking up the Arab,' said Morgan.

'They borrowed him, Joe. From the PLO or one of the Shi'ite groups. If you borrow a man, you have to

259

return him.' Reg looked round at Morgan's profile. 'Cheer up, you old eagle! She'll be all right.'

'She's a hostage, Reg.'

'Hostages lose their value if you kill them. All the Arab wants to do is get himself over the border. The CIA runs half the world from Switzerland. He knows he'll get looked after.'

Morgan and Reg had pulled up on a grass track under a grotesque baroque memorial fifty yards round the corner from where Roundie was parked; Toni and his squadron were covering Roundie's three likely exit roads.

'What the hell's he waiting for?' asked Toni over the walkie-talkie.

'A timed rendezvous,' said Morgan, 'maybe a couple of miles away.' He looked at his watch. 'A quarter or half past five, I'd guess.'

And so indeed it was – a puff of diesel exhaust came from the Mercedes at 17.10; it turned round at the traffic light in front of the palace and went back up the boulevard onto the *superstrada* heading north for the lake and the mountains.

One or two bonfires were already lit for the night. It was at the remains of last night's fire that Roundie turned off the road, bumping across the rough ground to where the motor caravan was parked. The car hardly stopped. The Arab walking from the caravan to climb into the passenger seat. Roundie was back on the road and heading north before Reg was even in sight.

Toni marked the spot until they arrived. Morgan ran for the caravan as soon as Reg pulled up. He saw a man stumble down the steps of the caravan and fall to his knees on the ground – presumably the taxi-driver.

Laleh was crouched on the floor inside, covered in blood and something worse than blood. She was whimpering like a child. Morgan knelt down beside her.

'If you're chasing your fat man,' said Reg's voice behind him, 'then go.' Reg took a towel from the basin and wiped Laleh's face. 'I'll look after her.' She dropped the car keys into his hand.

If Morgan had realized for how long his life would be conditioned by the events of the next two hours, would he have stepped back and paused?

Spread out under the hills, radio contact was suddenly very sporadic. Roundie was travelling very fast, already ten or fifteen minutes ahead, and Toni had not yet organized a link with Morgan on the walkie-talkie.

At the Lecco/Erba junction, Morgan had to take a chance. Roundie could have taken either road, he thought, as he hustled the eager little Alfa at twice the legal limit round the ninety-degree bend onto the Lecco road. The American with his borrowed killer might have doubled back to the *autostrada* at Como; or aimed over the top for Bellagio and the car ferry to the Lugano road on the other side of the lake.

Morgan was into the outskirts of Lecco and convinced he'd made a mistake before Toni crackled into life over the walkie-talkie. Toni was on the far side of the town, heading up the eastern shore of the lake, the other two in contact with the Mercedes six miles ahead.

The early evening, still light, was closing in. The storm promised by last night's taxi-driver breaking somewhere beyond them at the head of the lake. There was dark cloud; the first drops of rain on the windscreen as Morgan passed the Moto Guzzi boat-house short of Mandello. There's snow higher up, thought Morgan, feeling a sudden chill through the air vents. Autumn's threshold.

Turn back, one half of him was saying. Look after Laleh. Forget your anger.

The walkie-talkie crackled again at Colico. Roundie was already through Chiavenna, his last card played. 'He's going for the Splügen,' said Toni. 'If it's not snowed out.' Toni's ride was over. A frontier cul-de-sac and the risk of road-blocks were not for him or his two comrade companions, their faces and fingerprints on file.

'Telephone the border guards,' Morgan told him. 'Make out you're someone official and tell them to hold the white Mercedes – an Arab without a passport and carrying a gun.'

The ferocity of the storm higher up had turned rock-faces into waterfalls, the hairpin road into a torrent. The Mercedes and the Alfa were ten miles apart and alone on the pass, zigzagging on the old mule-track up the sheer sides of a mountain, and through tunnels where the water rushed like a city sewer.

Until, without warning, they'd climbed clear of it all at six thousand feet up out of the rain into mist, and then back into brilliant sunshine above the weather.

'Frontier,' said Roundie as they reached the dam on the plateau and the lake beyond. 'Ditch the gun.' They waited for the road to cross one of the feeder streams, then the Arab with reluctance flung his weapon from the bridge into the water.

A mile or two further on they reached the little hamlet huddled under the pass, grey slate roofs, and a handful of houses already boarded up for the winter. Another half-dozen hairpins and they were at the checkpoint, the red and white barrier across the road under the snow shed. The snowline was only a hundred yards or so above them.

A couple of young armed soldiers walked from the guardhouse. Roundie lowered his window into the cold thin wind with a laughing grin. '*Buona sera! Guten Abend! Bonsoir!* Good evening!' He handed them his passport. The guard flicked through it, then stooped to look through the car at the Arab on the far side.

'*Passaporto, prego. Dokumente, bitte. Passeport.* Your passport, if you please.' All said in deliberate parody of Roundie but without the hint of a smile.

262

'We've been over on a day trip. My friend left his papers at home. We're from Zurich. They let him through at Chiasso on the way in.'

The second guard walked slowly round the car and nodded at the Arab to climb out. Roundie opened his door. The first guard blocked it.

'*Lei non si muove.*' He gestured at Roundie to turn his engine off.

The second guard frisked the Arab against the car and opened the rear door and boot to search the entire vehicle. Without result. The Arab was nodded back into the car.

Somewhere far below along the lake they could hear the sound of another car, the rorty exhaust of Reg's Alfa echoing through the shuttered hamlet as Morgan attacked the final hairpins. Roundie was watching in his mirror as headlights drove over the brow and in under the snow shed alongside them.

Morgan clambered out of the Alfa, showing his ID to the guards. He'd had no clear idea what he was going to do – except keep moving one step ahead of *carabinieri* and *polizia* and beyond the reach of Elgin's orders. He didn't suppose Roundie would allow him to move them very far in any direction before forcing the showdown. As Morgan climbed into the back of the Mercedes, Roundie turned without much of a smile. 'Quite the little cowboy, Mr Hunter-Brown.'

Morgan nodded over his shoulder. 'Back down the hill, Mr Curtiss.'

The two guards were still standing there watching, Sten guns slung.

Roundie reversed the car slowly out of the shed and swung round, back down the hairpins, through the grey little hamlet at the foot of the hill and out along the lake towards the dam at the far end. Half a mile beyond the hamlet he coasted the car into the side of the road.

'Wrong move, Mr Hunter-Brown.' He looked up at Morgan in the driving mirror. 'It's two against one and you don't even carry a gun.' Roundie turned to the Arab. 'Drown him in the lake, Geronimo. They won't find him till the spring.'

The Arab pulled down his sun vizor to look at Morgan in the vanity mirror.

'Drown him in the water,' repeated Roundie.

Morgan spoke to the Arab, watching him through the mirror. 'Back up the road you're two minutes out of Switzerland. But you won't get into Switzerland without this.' Morgan pulled the Arab's passport from his inside pocket. 'And even with this, you won't get out of Italy without my say-so.'

'There's a hundred ways out of Italy,' laughed Roundie.

'If you go back down the mountain,' said Morgan, 'you'll find half the Italian police waiting for you.' Morgan's eyes held the killer's in the mirror. 'Waiting for *you*, not for him.'

'It's two against one against him,' said Roundie, his voice a little louder. 'Or it's two against one against you, you dumb Arab.' Roundie looked over his shoulder at Morgan. 'You want to kill the killer, Mr Hunter-Brown?'

Morgan was still watching the Arab. 'You're two minutes away from Switzerland,' he repeated quietly.

The Arab moved suddenly, reaching across Roundie to take the ignition key. He climbed out, walked round the front of the car and opened Roundie's door.

'Are you crazy?' shouted Roundie. 'Do you know who I am?'

The Arab chopped one hand into Roundie's midriff. The American doubled up in his seat, gasping for breath. The Arab pulled him from the car and turned him, both arms gripped high behind his shoulders; then walked him stumbling down the bank towards the water.

Morgan did not move from the back seat. Through the open car door he could hear a very distant sound of music – the hotel bar in the hamlet, he thought, and he looked round at the distant huddle of grey roofs. No sign of anyone. The houses and the circle of snow-dusted peaks were reflected in the water of the lake. The reflection was suddenly broken as the Arab reached the water. Roundie was struggling now, the Arab walking him out, up to his knees, up to his waist, finally with a sharp movement that seemed to break his arms and neck, pushing him under the water as though drowning a large puppy. The Arab held him there for a long time, ignoring the cold and the ice that had crept out from the shoreline on the north-facing side. When he turned away and walked out of the water, Roundie had disappeared.

Again Morgan glanced back at the hamlet where, apart from the distant sound of music, there was no sign of living souls, no one to watch the Arab as he returned up the bank to the road. The killer swung himself, dripping wet, into the driving seat and looked up at Morgan through the mirror. Morgan dropped the passport onto the front seat beside him and turned his head away. If it had been vengeance, there was little sweet about it.

He watched the hamlet carefully as the Arab turned the car back along the lakeside. Each house was boarded and shuttered; only the hotel and its bar were open – and facing the wrong way for anyone to have seen anything.

Two hundred yards above on the summit of the pass, the same pair of waiting frontier guards were surprised when the Arab produced his passport. They subjected it to minute scrutiny then looked over the roof of the car at Morgan for confirmation. Morgan had climbed out, feeling his legs weak and his head trembling. He nodded at the guards and the younger of them raised the barrier to let the Arab pass.

Morgan caught the young guard's eye as the barrier swung back down. 'He never spoke,' said Morgan in English. 'Not once.'

'*Prego?*' The guard had not understood.

'It doesn't matter.' Morgan turned back to the Alfa. The white Mercedes was already out of sight across the summit and into Switzerland. The moment he sat down in the car, Morgan felt himself begin to shake.

He stopped the car short of the lake in the grey-roofed hamlet and sat himself down in the hotel bar with a bottle of grappa, wondering if 'Roundie' Ralph Curtiss had a wife and kids.

14

The hotel was scrupulously clean, the cooking *casalinga*, the bedrooms sweet-smelling pinewood and Morgan, if not exactly drunk, certainly in no mood or mind to return to the world below.

He telephoned Milan: Laleh was unharmed but under sedation in a clinic, Reg told him. 'And where are you?' she asked, 'and where's my car?' Morgan would not say.

Perhaps if he'd known how and by whom pursuit had begun he would not have lingered in that high mountain hamlet seven thousand feet in the sky. But linger he did, watching each evening and morning between bottles of wine as the ice crept out further across the surface of the lake.

The white Mercedes had been found on the Tuesday morning by the Swiss police, abandoned and illegally parked outside the station in Thusis. 'They', the pursuers – the hunters or the hounds – arrived in Thusis that same afternoon to follow up inquiries and discovered a booking-clerk on the station who remembered the Arab catching the last-but-one train down the valley to Chur on Monday night. At Chur 'they' were told the Arab had bought a ticket to Basel; and at Basel a waitress recalled the Arab eating steak tartare in the first-class buffet on the station twenty minutes before it closed for the night. But no one had seen which of a dozen night trains he had then boarded. In that direction the trail seemed to fade.

In the other direction, 'they' returned to unravel the trail backwards from Thusis and eventually arrived on the Splügen at lunchtime on Wednesday, a couple of jerkined thirty-year-olds in a covered Jeep with a Zurich registration. They asked questions at the frontier checkpoint up on the pass, but both the Swiss and Italian guards involved on the Monday evening were off-duty and down in their respective valleys. The two thirty-year-olds parked their Jeep in the hamlet by the lake below the pass and, finding the hotel open, bought beers at the bar, Morgan, alone in the large dining room next door, listened to them as he ate his polenta and jugged hare.

They introduced themselves to the hotel owner as journalists – Panmeridian Press, Morgan wondered? It was fortunate that the hotel proprietor had taken a liking to Morgan; even more fortunate that he now took an instant dislike to the two newcomers and told them next to nothing at all: no, he had seen no Arab; and he had seen no jolly, corpulent American; and no, there had been no strangers on the pass since a half-dozen joyriders on Sunday.

When 'they' had driven away in their covered Jeep, he came through to the dining room with an opened bottle of Sasella and a wink for Morgan. 'I don't consider you a stranger,' he said.

'They'll be back,' Morgan warned him. 'Today, tomorrow, next week – but they will be back.'

'And when they do return?' The proprietor smiled. He was, Morgan thought, the healthiest man he'd ever seen, honed by clean air and altitude and quite uninterested in the other worlds that started down in the valley.

'They might come with photographs for you to identify,' said Morgan.

268

The proprietor shrugged and poured two glasses of wine. 'I never was much good at faces.'

That evening it began to snow, and a platoon of Alpine soldiers on exercise came down from their tents on the ridge to sing mountain songs with the frontier guards in the bar. And thus it was that Reg in a borrowed car found Morgan, alone in the empty dining room listening to the singing in the bar next door.

Reg sat with him and eventually asked him what had happened. She knew him well enough to know there was something he was trying to drown in the grappa and the wine.

'The killer killed his keeper,' Morgan replied, and told her blow by blow exactly what had happened.

'Why did you let the Arab go?' she asked him.

'I'd given him my word.'

Reg laughed. 'You're a bloody fool,' she said. 'They don't like losing men. They'll find the Arab and they'll make him talk before they kill him. And then, *caro mio*, "they" will come hunting for you.'

The road was a white ribbon in front of them as they left the hamlet. The headlights of both cars passed over the surface of the lake. The patches of ice on the far side had gathered the snow and, in contrast, the blackness of the water on the near side seemed malevolent. Was there a hand rising through the surface to point an accusing finger?

They went to collect Laleh from the clinic next day. Morgan sat on her bed while Reg waited in the car outside.

'Be gentle with her,' Reg had told Morgan. 'Your Mrs Colraine needs someone to put an arm round her.' It appeared that Cal, loud in complaint against the CIA, had been recalled for a debriefing in Washington.

Morgan stroked Laleh's hair and cheek.

'I thought if Parviz was with me he would be safe,'

269

she whispered to him. 'Roundie told me the address. He *wanted* me to be there.'

'He knew Parviz would come out if you were there,' said Morgan. 'It wasn't Cal – you know that, don't you?'

'I don't know anything,' she said, 'except that they were all betrayed and killed.'

'Cal had nothing to do with it,' Morgan repeated. 'You have to believe that.'

'Stay with me while I get dressed,' she said.

In the car Laleh stared from the window at wet Milan streets. 'The English girl and her father came to see me,' she said. 'They wanted to know how Parviz had died.'

Reg was watching her in the mirror; they were stationary at a traffic light.

'He was sitting next to me reciting a poem,' said Laleh. 'It was as though he knew it was going to happen.'

Reg walked them to the check-in at the airport. The two women embraced when they said goodbye.

'Do you have a home to go to?' asked Reg, turning to Morgan. She gave him a peck on the cheek. 'See you next year or the year after,' she said. 'Or the year after that.'

Laleh held his hand on the plane and eventually, as Morgan knew she would, asked him what had happened.

'The Arab escaped into Switzerland and Roundie disappeared,' said Morgan with approximate accuracy.

Laleh held his hand again in the car from Heathrow and raised it once to her lips before disengaging as the cab passed Shepherd's Bush. She was, Morgan recognized, preparing herself to re-enter her own world – her refuge in these neat London streets whose sheltered trees and gardens had not yet finished their summer.

Morgan paid off the taxi at her gate in the hope she would ask him to stay. He felt a warmth for her, an affinity – two displaced persons in their displaced worlds. He wanted to share some of that warmth.

Laleh found her key in her bag and turned to Morgan in the opened door. 'My mother married one passport,' she said. 'I have two. I need security. This is my home.' She held out her hand. 'Goodbye, Joe.'

Laleh watched him from the sitting-room window as he walked away through the gate, swinging his black canvas bag, across the road and under the trees along the canal. She thought him the most isolated man she'd ever known. His aloneness and self-sufficiency frightened her. She too would have liked to share warmth.

The door of Rudi's flat was repaired and locked and neither 'oral French' nor 'schoolgirl' answered.

Morgan found his brother at the jazz pub – the sound of 'Basin Street Blues' down St Martin's Lane. Morgan watched through the side window by the door – Beth was playing cards in the corner; and Rudi was happy enough as he blew his long wailing solo. Why disturb him again?

Morgan looked at his watch. He'd just about make the evening boat-train from Victoria; Lille by early morning; Basel by mid-afternoon; fried eggs on melted cheese and a bottle of Fendant in the Swiss restaurant car; and back to Frau Luethi's *pensione* in Lugano by early evening.

Railway Joe was going 'home'.